HOW WAS IT FOR YOU, PROFESSOR?

Also by William Hartston

The Drunken Goldfish:
A Celebration of Irrelevant Research

William Hartston

How Was It For You, Professor?

A Celebration of Sex Research

Grafton
An Imprint of HarperCollins*Publishers*

Grafton
An Imprint of HarperCollins*Publishers,*
77–85 Fulham Palace Road,
Hammersmith, London W6 8JB

A Grafton Original 1992
9 8 7 6 5 4 3 2 1

A catalogue record for this book is
available from the British Library

ISBN 0 586 21487 9

Set in Palatino

Printed in Great Britain by
HarperCollinsManufacturing Glasgow

Contents

How Was It For You, Professor?

A celebration of sex research
by William Hartston

'The author, with his hands washed, inserted his lubricated index and/or middle fingers into the subject's vagina and proceeded to systematically friction both vaginal walls, applying a moderate to strong rhythmic pressure at an angle to the wall, going from the lower to the upper half of the vagina, and starting at the posterior wall. The subject was asked to indicate the sensations, erotic or other, she was experiencing in the different stimulated zones, and when a region of increasing erotic sensitivity was found, increasingly stronger pressure was applied until either the subject reached orgasm or the examiner's fatigue made him stop stimulation. In order to record more precisely some subjects' responses, a second examination was conducted on several subjects.'

H.Alzate, 'Vaginal Eroticism: A Replication Study'
(see chapter 5)

Acknowledgements

Normal standards of decency, the laws of libel and the fifth amendment to the American constitution preclude my giving credit to all those who have stimulated my interest and assisted my research into this complex and sometimes sticky area.

None of this would have been possible without the efforts of the many dedicated researchers who have, in their unending quest for knowledge, dedicatedly watched pornographic movies and soiled the sheets of academia before me. Their findings have been laboriously collated in the pages of such academic publications as *Archives of Sexual Behavior* and the *Journal of Sex Research*, to whose editors and publishers I am greatly indebted.

I must also register my gratitude to Merlin Unwin, who was present at the conception of the work, and was the first to appreciate its potential, before he went off to do something connected with fish.

Ian Paten then re-awakened my academic concupiscence and, with the assistance of Sheila Watson's gentle bullying, eased the manuscript through its slow gestation.

Val Hudson bought me lunch and I had the salmon *en croute* with chips, so I'd like to thank her too.

William Hartston
London and Cambridge
1992

Author's Foreplay

As Baumeister (1988) pointed out, 'performing oral sex does not require high level choice or complex abstract thought'. Why then, you will surely be asking, have academics been so slow to share with ordinary people their knowledge of sex, either oral or in written form?

When Wheeler and Rubin (1987) wrote their classic paper, 'A Comparison of Volumetric and Circumferential Measures of Penile Erection', why were their important findings not made more generally available? Did they not consider that amateur sex practitioners might like to know which was the best measure of penis size to predict sexual arousal levels?

Indeed, why, after more than a quarter of a century of successful use in academic laboratories, is such a simple device as a penile tumescence gauge not freely available across the counter in Woolworths?

The answers to these and countless similar questions are not easy. Academic researchers are a shy and cautious breed, wary of making claims that might prove to be unjustified. It could be said that in the field of sex research, that caution is well advised. They are, after all, in the vast majority of cases dealing with samples of volunteer subjects who are exposing their responses to erotic stimuli, or admitting their sexual preferences, in laboratory conditions, with people watching.

It could be argued that male subjects who are faced with visually presented erotic stimuli, while having penile tumescence gauges attached to their private parts, knowing that scientists are recording their every twitch, may not react in a manner typical of the average man watching the same dirty videos in the privacy of his own front room. Or that female subjects who volunteer to have a heated oxygen electrode measure the haemodynamic changes of their vaginas may not be typical of the general population.

Such arguments are well-known to all researchers in the behavioural sciences, but they are the objections of philistines who would retard the pace of progress and hamper the development of knowledge.

As the reader will see, sex research has, largely over the past two decades, made some significant discoveries with considerable life-enhancing potential which have been recorded in the pages of such specialist publications as the *Journal of Sex Research* and *Archives of Sexual Behavior*.

For the first time, this book collates the findings of dedicated sex researchers in some of the world's greatest universities, and presents them in a form readily accessible to the general public. For the first time, you have in your hands a compendium of sex techniques and knowledge that have been academically verified. I trust you will find it a pleasurable and worthwhile romp through the world of academic sex research.

References

Baumeister, R.F. (1988): *Masochism and the Self.*

Wheeler, D. and Rubin, H.B. (1987): 'A comparison of volumetric and circumferential measures of penile erection'. *Archives of Sexual Behav.* (16) 289–99.

1

Joy of Man's Desiring

This textbook is intended primarily for the participant or would-be participant in sexual activity who wishes to discover a little more before launching into what is, after all, a complex subject. Before starting anything, however, we should pause to establish our criteria of success.

It is widely known that the pursuit of sexual activity can involve the expenditure of vast amounts of energy, time and perhaps even money. What is going to make those investments worthwhile? In these opening two chapters, we shall see what progress has been made by researchers into establishing an objective measure of the degree of sexual satisfaction a person is feeling.

In the old days of empirical sociology, self-reporting was widely used in such circumstances, but such data are, by their very nature, subjective, and hence unreliable. It is all very well thinking one is enjoying oneself, but how can one be sure? As we shall see, using simple devices such as a strain gauge attached to the penis or a heated electrode in the vagina, readings may be taken that give reliable information.

To avoid any possible confusion, we should point out here that in the title of this chapter, the words 'Joy', 'Man' and 'Desiring' should be taken to refer explicitly and exclusively to the pleasures of the male participating in sexual activity. The vexed questions of whether the experimenter is feeling desires or joy, and whether he ought to be doing so, will be discussed in chapter 5.

In discussing male sexual arousal (which we shall take to be, in non-deviant cases at least, a precondition for enjoyment), we must be clear about the distinction between psychological arousal and physiological arousal. For a clarification of this important issue, we are indebted to Mosher, Barton-Henry and Green (1988) who lucidly state: 'Subjective sexual arousal is defined as an affect-cognition blend in consciousness of awareness of physiological sexual arousal and sexual affects or affect-cognition blends (that is, sexual interest, sexual enjoyment, sexual pleasure, or anticipatory excitement).'

It is difficult to disagree with that statement. Indeed, it

Awareness of physiological sexual arousal

is difficult to understand it at all. We shall return later to their investigations on subjective arousal of 120 male and 121 female undergraduates at the University of Connecticut. For the moment, let us proceed with the physiological symptoms.

Ever since the discovery of Sex as an academic pursuit (by Kinsey et al in 1948, and later again by Masters and Johnson in 1966), it has been generally agreed that it results in an increase in size in the penis.

But do penises that start large grow more, inch for inch, than those that start small, and does it matter? Since these questions could be important in calibrating any device that is designed to measure arousal, we shall start by reviewing the findings.

At Kinsey's request, more than 3,500 upstanding Americans got out their tape-measures and recorded the length along the top of their penis from belly to tip. Masters and Johnson described the comparable measurement as 'from the anterior border of the symphasis at the base of the penis along the dorsal surface to the distal tip of the glans', but perhaps their subjects preferred longer words.

Anyway, they asked for measurements in flaccid and erect states, and also for the maximum circumference measurement in both states. On Kinsey's figures, penis length increased on average 63.4 per cent and circumference increased 32 per cent on erection.

The average figures (the units are inches) were as shown in the table below:

	Flaccid	*Erect*
Length	3.89	6.21
Circumference	3.75	4.85

Kinsey, however, looked only at the overall picture, not separating small penises from large ones. That task was left to Masters and Johnson (1966) who hand-picked two groups each of 40 men, selected for below-average or above-average penis lengths. Their intention was to test the 'phallic fallacy' that large flaccid penises grow more proportionately than smaller ones.

Their results contradicted that hypothesis, but it was another twenty-one years before Jamison and Gebhard (1987) showed that in fact the opposite is the case: out of small penises, large erections grow.

They went back to Kinsey's original data using some clever statistical methods to adjust for possible bias in the sample. Of all the men interviewed by Kinsey, only a half had measured their penis for him. During the interviews, however, all had given an estimate of their penis size. By comparing penis-measurers with non-measurers, and estimates with measurements, Jamison and Gebhard were able to correct their figures for sample bias.

The men who returned measurements, incidentally, were 0.15 inches taller and 2 pounds lighter on average than those who did not. It may therefore be inferred, with some confidence, that tall thin men are more likely to measure their penises for a researcher than short fat ones.

On partitioning the subjects into two groups corresponding to short (<3.5 inches) and long (>4 inches) flaccid penises, the results were unmistakable. As a percentage of flaccid penis length, the average erectile increase in the short group was 86.6 per cent compared with a mere 47.7 per cent for the long ones. The comparable scores on circumference were 37.6 per cent versus 28.4 per cent.

So the result seems proven at last: small penises do indeed grow more, inch for inch, than long ones. And a consequence of this is that there is a greater spread of sizes among flaccid penises than erect ones. Which could in part account for the frequently quoted view that 'size is not important'.

There is, however, one methodological consideration which appears not to have been taken into account, and which could provide an alternative explanation of the results: can we be sure that all subjects adopted the same measuring strategy?

Suppose some subjects, in their enthusiasm to obtain a correct reading of their flaccid penis lengths, applied a slight stretching to the organ in question in an attempt to render it true and straight, while others simply took the readings in a natural state. Might it not then also be a reasonable hypothesis that men with small penises were more likely, in the interests of accuracy, to apply additional stretching to iron out the wrinkles?

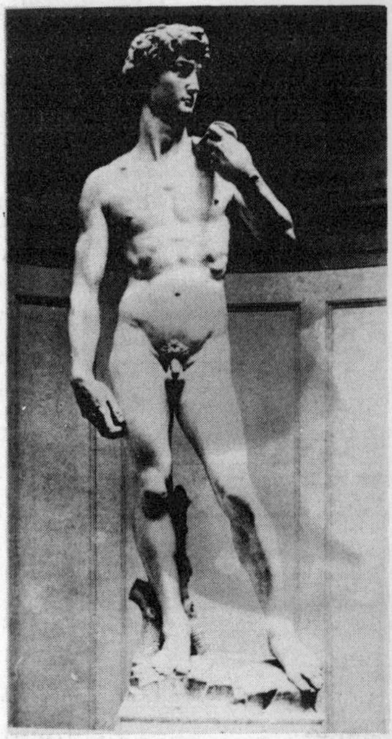

Men with small penises . . .

If this is indeed what happened, then some of the supposedly large flaccid penises in the study would have been merely stretched small ones, with not much further to go when erect. The smaller increases in size recorded, therefore, could have been an artefact of the measuring strategy rather than a general property of large penises.

In order to obtain more reliable data, each man's penis would have to be measured by an independent observer or, better still, by a group of different observers independently.

Returning to the subject of importance of size, we cannot leave without mentioning another valuable piece of recent research. Fisher, Branscombe and Lemery (1983) presented female subjects with erotic stimuli (also known as dirty pictures) involving a variety of penis sizes, both flaccid and erect. Their conclusion was that the arousal value of the pictures, as measured by the subjects' own responses, was not at all dependent on penis length.

'That's all very well,' I hear you say. 'But how do I measure how much bigger my penis is getting without having to whip out a tape-measure every few seconds which could easily interfere with whatever else I'm doing at the time?'

A good question, to which there are two primary answers, as outlined by Wheeler and Rubin (1987) in their excellent discussion of whether it is better to try to measure the volume or circumference of a growing penis.

The simplest method is a strain gauge transducer, which you make by filling a 30 cm length of Silastic tubing (0.5 mm interior diameter) with mercury. You then seal both ends with platinum electrodes, rubber cement and shrinkable tubing. This mercury-filled tube is then attached to a piece of plastic to form a loop, 3 cm in circumference, which may be placed around the penis. The loop then forms a bridge in an electric circuit through which a steady current of one volt is passed. As the enclosed penis changes size, the loop stretches and its electrical resistance is affected.

'The loop then forms a bridge in an electric circuit'

An ammeter's readings can thus be interpreted as a measure of penis circumference. By connecting a pen and graph paper to the whole contraption, we can thus record penis changes throughout an experimental session.

The other method is more fiddly and was first described in Freund, Sedlacek and the delightfully named

Knob in their 1965 paper 'A Simple Transducer for Mechanical Plethysmography of the Male Genital'.

Their idea was to measure the change in volume of the penis by enclosing it in an elastic tube connected to an airtight diaphragm over a glass cylinder. The whole thing was put together in a way that ensured that any increase in penis size would stretch the rubber and result in an increase in pressure inside the cylinder.

What Wheeler and Rubin did was to compare these two devices by having subjects watch dirty films while wearing both of them simultaneously.

'Stimuli consisted of two commercially available erotic motion pictures of approximately 10 minutes duration recorded on videotape. The content of the stimuli consisted of a variety of explicit heterosexual and lesbian behaviors.'

To make sure that their subjects' attentions did not wander from the videos, they arranged that a brief flash of light would occur at random intervals, about once every fifteen seconds, at the top or bottom of the screen. The subject had to press a button by his left hand whenever the light flashed.

Each subject went into a private booth ('in which the ambient temperature was maintained at about 27° C'), where he was given instructions on how to attach one rubber ring to the base of his penis and then insert the whole organ into another rubber tube which finally had to be connected to a nipple on a cylinder.

Then he watched the film three times, being told to relax and enjoy it on the first and third times, while on the second showing he was instructed 'to inhibit erection by any means possible except by not looking at the film'.

As he watched the film, the experimental paraphernalia would record every twitch of his penis.

And what it all showed was that the strain gauge was just as good as the more complicated volumetric device, which seemed remarkably prone to leaks and unreliable readings caused by the subject's bodily movements. Other researchers, however, while agreeing that the volumetric device is a pain to work with, still believe that it gives better results if it does not fall apart.

For the beginner we have no hesitation in recommending the strain gauge. And that brings us to the question of how to use it.

'There are presently three widely used methods of scoring penile circumferential data', Earls, Quinsey and Castonguay (1987) tell us at the beginning of their paper. The simplest is just to measure the number of millimetres change in the circumference of the penis. This gives a simple score for enlargement. A little more complicated, but fairer to people with small penises, is to consider any reading within a series of trials as a percentage of the maximum expansion obtained. The scores will then range from 0 (flaccid) to 100 (fully erect) for everyone.

Finally, the complicated way is to make a z-score transformation. This is a tricky statistical procedure which takes into account all the scores over a session and reduces them to a standard form around an average of zero and with a standard deviation of one.

Earls, Quinsey and Castonguay had their subjects put on the mercury-in-rubber strain gauges, then watch a sexually explicit videotape in order to establish the range between 0 per cent and 100 per cent erection. After being given time to recover, they got on with the main experiment.

> Stimuli were 20 photographic slides assigned to five categories of four slides each: adult female, adolescent female, adult male, adolescent male. Each slide presented a frontal view of a nude individual in a variety of positions. Four neutral stimuli depicting pastoral scenes of flowers and trees were also used.

What the results showed was that the z-scores gave a more statistically reliable picture of an individual's response pattern than either of the simpler measures, but whether it is worth the effort is doubtful.

The experimenters do not mention whether any of the subjects were particularly aroused by flowers or trees.

Finger temperature as a measure of sexual arousal

Finally, we must mention a little-known piece of research which should be of interest to anyone who feels uncomfortable sticking his penis into a mercury-in-rubber strain gauge.

In 1976, Kabbash, Brender and Bowman in their paper 'Finger Temperature as a Measure of Sexual Arousal in Males and Females' demonstrated that finger temperature may be a measure of sexual arousal in males and females. The idea is simple: since sexual arousal results in, and erection is caused by, increased blood flowing into the genitals, it makes sense to hypothesize that if there is more blood in the genitals, there must be less in the finger-tips, and finger temperature would go down as sexual arousal went up.

This indeed proved to be the case. The three researchers took the temperature of subjects' fingers as they watched neutral, moderately erotic or highly erotic videotapes. (The erotic intensity of the tapes had previously been assessed by an independent group of observers.) Their fingers were colder when watching erotic than non-erotic tapes, and colder when watching very erotic, than when watching mildly erotic.

Also, it was shown that their finger temperature was lower

when actually watching dirty movies than when thinking about watching dirty movies. And all of this applied to both men and women.

References and further reading

Barlow, D.H., Becker, R., Leitenberg, H. and Agras, W.S. (1970): 'A mechanical strain gauge for recording penile circumference change'. *J. App. Behav. Anal.* (3) 73–6.

Earls, C.M., Quinsey, V.L. and Castonguay, L.G. (1987): 'A comparison of three methods of scoring penile circumference changes'. *Archives of Sexual Behav.* (16) 493–500.

Fisher, W.A., Branscombe, N.R. and Lemery, C.R. (1983): 'The bigger the better? Arousal and attributional responses to erotic stimuli that depict different size of penises'. *J. Sex Research* (19) 377–96.

Freund, K., Sedlacek, F. and Knob, K. (1965): 'A simple transducer for mechanical plethysmography of the male genital'. *J. Exp. Anal. Behav.* (8) 169–70.

Graber, B., Rohrbaugh, J.W., Dewlin, D.B., Varner, J.L. and Ellington, R.J. (1985): 'EEG during masturbation and ejaculation'. *Archives of Sexual Behav.* (14) 491–503.

Jamison, P.L. and Gebhard, P.H. (1987): 'Penis size increase between flaccid and erect states: an analysis of the Kinsey data'. *J. Sex Research* (24) 177–83.

Kabbash, L., Brender, W. and Bowman, T. (1976): 'Finger temperature as a measure of sexual arousal in males and females'. In *Progress in Sexology* (Ed. R. Gemme), Plenum Press.

Kinsey, A.C., Pomeroy, W.B. and Martin, C.E. (1948): *Sexual Behaviour in the Human Male.* Saunders, Philadelphia.

Masters, W.H. and Johnson, V.E. (1966): *Human Sexual Response.* Little, Brown & Co., Boston.

McConaghy, N. (1967): 'Penile volume change to moving pictures of male and female nudes in heterosexual and homosexual males'. *Behav. Res. and Ther.* (5) 43–8.

Mosher, D.L., Barton-Henry, M. and Green, S.E. (1988): 'Subjective sexual arousal and involvement: Development of multiple indicators'. *J. Sex Research* (24) 412–25.

Rosen, C. and Keefe, F.J. (1978): 'The measurement of human penile tumescence'. *Psychophysiology* (15) 366–76.
Wheeler, D. and Rubin, H.B. (1978): 'A comparison of volumetric and circumferential measures of penile erection'. *Archives of Sexual Behav.* (16) 289–99.
Zuckerman, M. (1971): 'Physiological measures of sexual arousal in the human'. *Psychological Bull.* (75) 297–329.

2

Joy of Woman's Desiring

Not having penile adjuncts, women present a problem to the sex researcher. Basically, the difficulty is that one cannot conveniently wrap a rubber tube containing mercury around their sexual organs, nor can they profitably be encased in a rubber diaphragm.

For many years, subjective reports and orgasms were the only available measure of female sexual enjoyment, but this aspect of sexual science was revolutionized in 1970 (see Cohen and Shapiro, 1971), with the invention of the vaginal photoplethysmograph. This handy little device is a meter, in an acrylic holder clipped to a vaginal diaphragm, that measures blood flow across the vagina.

Before proceeding to a discussion of the uses of this elegant little thermoconductance flowmeter and a journey down the rapids of the trans-vaginal bloodstream, let us take a historical perspective of the whole subject.

Although female orgasm was first discovered by science in 1953 (when Kinsey's survey reported that 39 per cent of women achieved orgasm always or nearly always, while only about 5 per cent or 6 per cent never did) it is clear from historical evidence that women had probably been enjoying sex long before anyone thought to ask them about it.

In a seventeenth-century Somerset court statement, a witness said: 'I have fucked Kent's wife, the miller, to the flitters.' Since flitters, in seventeenth-century Somerset dialect, meant the state of shaking with nervous agitation or excitement, we consequently have assuredly a definite case of a seventeenth-century Somerset orgasm, perhaps the first on record in the west of England.

Recent studies with monkeys, however, have provided a strong argument that female orgasms may date back to an even earlier period of evolution.

In Zumpe and Michael (1968) the researcher followed the sexual adventures of three female rhesus monkeys (*Macaca mulatta*). They observed a clutching reaction by the hands that was identified as a sign of orgasm. In the course of the investigation, the three lady monkeys experienced 389 ejaculations from a variety of males. In 97 per cent of all cases, they exhibited the orgasmic clutching reflex.

Three years later, Burton (1971) went further by cutting the male monkey out of the fun. In his experiments, the female *Macaca mulatta* was brought to orgasm by stimulation of its clitoris and vagina by an artificial (monkey-) penis.

Oddly, no one appears to have cast doubt on the moral probity of a trio of girl monkeys who are willing to experience 389 ejaculations from a variety of males, or questioned the psychological state of one who allows her clitoris and vagina to be stimulated by a dildo-wielding scientist. There have, however, been some doubts cast on the credentials of women who allow vaginal photoplethysmographs to be clipped to their diaphragms.

In their survey 'Volunteer Bias in Research Employing Vaginal Measures of Sexual Arousal', Wolchik, Spencer and Lisi (1983) gave questionnaires to 296 female psychology students who had volunteered for a study on sexuality and personality. After completing the questionnaires, the subjects were given a written description of an experiment that involved sexually explicit videotapes and vaginal photoplethysmographs and were asked to indicate whether they would be interested in participating in the experiment.

The results showed that those who volunteer for such an experiment are more likely to enjoy dirty films, more likely to have suffered sexual trauma, less likely to have sexual fear and likely to masturbate more frequently than non-volunteers. The paper ends with a warning: *This study demonstrates that the external validity of studies employing vaginal measures of sexual arousal is limited. Researchers must use caution when discussing the generality of findings based on genital measurement of sexual arousal.*

Subsequent researchers appear to have taken little notice of the warning, continuing merrily to monitor vaginal blood flow in volunteer video watchers, perhaps because they feel that the findings of Wolchik, Spencer and Lisi may be considered suspect as they used volunteer subjects themselves.

What they had established was not the differences between people who volunteer for sex experiments and people who do not volunteer for sex experiments, but the difference between such volunteers and non-volunteers in a sample already biased by including only people who volunteered to complete questionnaires in the first place.

No doubt someone is, at this very moment, working on a piece of research which will lead to a paper entitled: 'Volunteer Bias in Research Employing Questionnaires on Volunteer Bias in Research Employing Vaginal Measures of Sexual Arousal'.

In fairness, however, we should take notice of Barker and Perlman (1975) who failed to find any significant personality differences between volunteers and non-volunteers for a sex survey. They gave 254 subjects (126 male and 128 female) a personality questionnaire (which they all filled in), then subsequently sent each of them a sex questionnaire.

Comparing those who returned the sex questionnaire with those who did not, failed to show any particular features that might characterize sex-test volunteers.

On the other hand, the whole sample of 254 subjects was taken from students enrolled on an introductory psychology course, so it is an open question whether the result generalizes to normal people.

While on the subject of methodological concerns, we should mention two other potential causes of inaccuracy that permeate the whole of this area of research. The first is the problem of motivational distortion, or fibbing, in answering questionnaires. Newcomer and Udry (1988) attempted to come to grips with this question by asking 1,152 adolescents whether they had been telling the truth when they replied to a survey on sexual intercourse two years previously.

Their results showed that 7 per cent admitted that they had lied in their responses and that another 'substantial proportion' seemed to be unclear about what they had said.

What this result tells us is obscure, since we do not know whether the 7 per cent were telling the truth about their lying. We also do not know whether those who said that they had told the truth were telling the truth second time around or not. And how many of that 'substantial proportion' did not want to confess that they remembered how they had answered two years before?

Secondly, we must consider the possible effects the experimenter has on his or her experimental subjects.

In an interesting study in 1988, Winer, Makowski, Alpert and Collins (1988) tested whether different experimenters obtained different results when administering the same questionnaire to matched groups of subjects.

The questions covered various aspects of general sexual attitudes and beliefs as well as specific individual behaviour. The experimenters in this study were a psychologist, a rabbi and a priest. Lest the subjects forget who they were dealing with, both the clerics came in their working clothes.

The first finding was that there was no significant difference between the rabbi and the priest as testers.

The second finding was that there was practically no difference between the clerics and the psychologist either. All the statistics revealed was a slight trend that more respondents admitted having had intercourse in the past month when a psychologist was asking the question than when a member of the clergy asked.

All of which has little to do with 'Patterns of Female Sexual Arousal During Sleep and Waking: Vaginal Thermo-Conductance Studies', by Fisher, Cohen, Schiava, Davis, Furman, Ward, Edwards and Cunningham, a veritable gang-bang of a research paper which showed that women, when sleeping, may experience something analogous to a male's erections.

Their idea was that men are known frequently to have erections while dreaming. Since dreaming sleep is characterized by rapid eye movements (REM) our researchers' plan was to monitor the vaginal blood flow (VBF) of sleeping women during REM sleep. The results would be compared with their VBF during waking periods of non-erotic and erotic stimulation. (They obtained these results by asking the subjects to masturbate and/or watch dirty movies.)

What they found was that with subjects awake, only erotic stimuli produced changes in vaginal blood flow, and that even at their greatest these were no greater than the VBF changes recorded during REM sleep.

Their conclusion that women may be erotically aroused when asleep received one further piece of confirmation when they recorded, in the course of their investigations, a single instance of a dream-produced orgasm. During a two-minute sleep period, the subject's heart rate increased from 50 to 100 a minute, and the respiratory rate from 12 to 22 a minute. The next morning, she reported her dream:

> I was being made love to by an older woman whom I did not recognize. I was passive while this woman kissed me a lot. I do not remember if I responded but I had a very good time. It was exciting. I believe the woman masturbated me externally but did not insert her finger. The weird and disturbing part of the dream was when I reached down after orgasm and discovered that it was

a man and not a woman. She had two penises, one was small and in the usual place and the other large like a breast in the groin.

The small penis was 'curled like a snake and looked disgusting'. The researchers have suggested that the experiment itself, particularly the women attendants, the erotic material read by the subject and the snake-like wires protruding from the VBF device may all have contributed to what was, for the subject, a highly atypical homosexual experience.

If, as appears to be the assumption underlying much of the research, orgasms are fun things for women to have, there is the question of what they really are and how many one should aim for. These matters were investigated by Amberson and Hoon (1985) the summary of which begins: 'Seventeen women masturbated to orgasm several times in succession while being measured intravaginally by a device that allows continuous oxygen and blood flow readings.'

The researchers were testing two hypotheses: 1) that the female physiological response will increase with sequential orgasms; 2) that women will subjectively recognize and report an increased intensity or pleasure with successive orgasms; i.e. that each orgasm is 1) stronger and 2) more fun than the one before.

It is important to point out here that they were investigating sequential, not multiple orgasm. As they point out: 'Sequential orgasm includes pauses between orgasmic responses and requires restimulation of the genitals every few minutes, whereas multiple orgasm involves continued stimulation and no break.'

Rather than using the basic photoplethysmograph of many earlier researchers (since doubt had been cast on its reliability at high levels of sexual excitement) they employed a heated oxygen electrode, mounted on the vaginal wall with a small amount of suction, to measure blood flow and oxygen levels.

With the instruments inserted, subjects (all white, middle-class, in administrative or professional careers, average age thirty) were offered the use of an electric vibrator (half accepted, the other half used their hands). They were instructed to relax, in privacy, and read the *National Geographic* magazine until the instrument readings settled down. They were then told to indulge in an erotic fantasy of their choice, and when completed to commence masturbation to orgasm. Then relax, fantasize and masturbate again. This went on until the subject decided she had had enough. 'After each orgasm, subjects were asked to rate subjective pleasure' on a scale from 1 to 7.

The experimenters report that: '*All 17 subjects reached orgasm once, 16 twice, 8 three times, 4 four times and 1 seven times. There were no significant differences between those using the vibrators and those using hands.*'

The results confirmed neither of the two original hypotheses, but suggested that one orgasm, in general, is about as strong and pleasurable as the one before or the one after.

. . . the other half used their hands

Their figures did, however, seem to show that the *National Geographic* magazine is not very exciting.

Geer and Quartararo (1976) carried on their investigations on seven female student subjects (three single, three divorced, one married) into the post-orgasmic phase. Their procedure was a variation of the now familiar one:

> The subject room . . . contained a reclining subject chair, two small tables, and an enclosed lavatory. The experimenter took the subject into the lavatory where she was shown the vaginal plethysmograph which was resting in a 750:1 solution of zepheran chloride. She was told to rinse the device in water, place it approximately one inch into the vagina, then walk to the subject chair, adjust the chair to desired position, plug the phone jack at the end of the device into a small box on one of the tables, and then indicate verbally over a continuous open intercom that she was ready.

When she was ready, the subject was told to rest for ten minutes, after which she was instructed to 'begin masturbation and to say "OK" when she experienced orgasm'.

After orgasm the subject remained resting for ten minutes while recordings continued. Then she could remove the device and come out of the room. An analysis of the results produced some intriguing findings:

> It is of considerable interest to note that for all subjects the vaginal pressure pulse and pooled blood volume remained elevated above baseline throughout the post-orgasm 10 minute period. Indeed, for some subjects, there was no diminishing of the vasocongestion even after 10 minutes had elapsed. It is tempting to suggest that this finding reflects the physiological basis for multiple orgasms in women and the general report that women maintain more interest in sexual contact immediately after

Plug the phone jack at the end of the device into a small box

orgasm than do men. Extreme caution needs to be exercised with such speculations.

The women, incidentally, took an average of 2 minutes 8 seconds to reach orgasm.

Whether there is more to female orgasm than just having fun was investigated by Cyril A. Fox in his 1976 paper, 'Orgasm and Fertility'. One part of his investigation was to consider whether orgasm is an aid to conception.

One suggestion, originally made in Fox, Wolff and Baker (1970), is that orgasm involves uterine contraction which can aid the transport of the sperm.

Another idea is connected with the vaginal pH value. 'It has often been stated', says Cyril Fox, 'that the vagina is a hostile environment for human semen since the former is at pH4 compared with the latter at pH7 (approximate figures). As spermatozoa are immobilized at pH6 or less, it follows that the quicker the semen enters the relatively alkaline uterus the better.'

Various reports have suggested that sexual stimulation increases the vaginal pH value, thus making it likely that female orgasm can speed up otherwise sluggish sperm.

'The balance, in terms of fertility, would appear to shift in favor of the orgasmic woman and the quality of the orgasm may be of significance.'

We cannot end this discussion, however, without a warning concerning the potential problems that may be associated with extremely fast-moving sperm. In his purely theoretical article, Milton Love (1983) hypothesizes sexual relations between the fictional characters Superman and Lois Lane:

> It is certainly well within the realms of possibility that these peristaltic, *involuntary* waves [created by the neuromuscular seizure of Superman's orgasm] caused by Superman's supermuscles, might propel his supersperm at incredible speeds . . . we might expect these sperm cells of steel to be propelled through the hapless partner, as well as the bed, floor and perhaps ultimately out of the Solar System.

If Miss Lane cannot take the precautionary measure of inserting a small piece of kryptonite at the base of Superman's penis, she might well, in view of Cyril Fox's conclusions, be advised not to risk making matters worse by reaching orgasm herself.

In a sense, however, we have started at the end of the story, for orgasm (and post-orgasmic vaginal blood volume) are the destination of the path of sexual enjoyment. To measure the effect of mounting the steps along that road, we need to be familiar with the work of Hoon, Hoon and Wincze (1976) who developed the Sexual Arousal Index for precisely that purpose.

Starting by reading various books, articles and magazines

on female sexuality, they drew up a list of 131 things that might arouse a woman. After 151 women had assessed how much they were aroused by each description, they analysed the results and found that there were five separate dimensions of erotic arousability:

1 Foreplay – dancing, kissing, caressing
2 Vicarious arousal – looking at dirty pictures, reading dirty books
3 Breast stimulation
4 Intercourse – preparation and participation
5 Genital stimulation by partner or of partner

With these factors identified, the original 131 items were then reduced to 28, by selecting those most representative of each factor. So on the final Sexual Arousal Index, the respondent will find items such as:

1 When a loved one stimulates your genitals with mouth and tongue
7 When you caress a loved one's genitals with your fingers
17 When you hear sounds of pleasure during sex
19 When you read suggestive or pornographic poetry
25 When a loved one fondles your breasts with mouth and tongue
27 When you masturbate

and each item must be rated on a scale from −1 to 5 as follows:

−1 adversely affects arousal – unthinkable, repulsive, distracting
0 doesn't affect sexual arousal
1 possibly causes sexual arousal
2 sometimes causes sexual arousal – slightly arousing
3 usually causes sexual arousal – moderately arousing
4 almost always sexually arousing – very arousing
5 always causes sexual arousal – extremely arousing

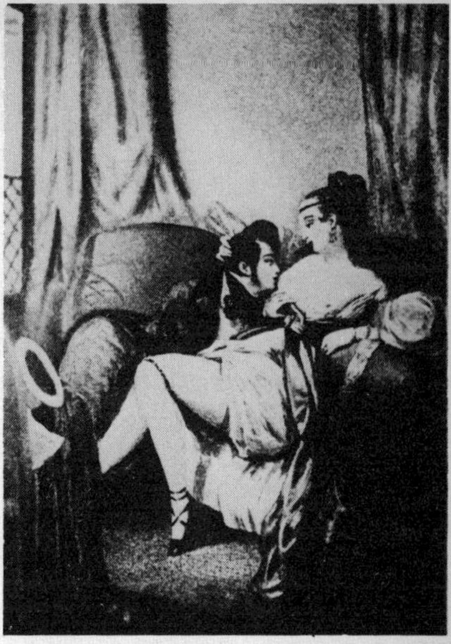

When a loved one fondles your breasts with mouth and tongue

A woman's total score on the Index is simply the sum of the numbers chosen for all of the 28 items, so a woman disgusted by everything will score −28, while one who finds everything extremely arousing would score 140.

And what the test showed was that women with high Sexual Arousal Index scores tend to be older, better educated and have more children than low scorers, and they are also more sexually satisfied, more aware of physiological changes during arousal, have intercourse more before and during marriage, have more orgasms during intercourse, and have more orgasms during masturbation.

Finally, before leaving female orgasms, we must mention McLean et al (1983), who reported a case of a woman taking a drug for depression who asked for further supplies of the drug, even after she was cured. She admitted that while taking the drug, every time she yawned, she experienced orgasm. An analogous effect was also reported in a male patient on the same drug.

Whether either of them subscribed to the *National Geographic* magazine for its potential yawn-inducing value was not reported.

References and further reading

Amberson, J.I. and Hoon, P.W. (1985): 'Hemodynamics of sequential orgasm'. *Archives of Sexual Behav.* (14) 351–60.

Barker, W.J. and Perlman, D. (1975): 'Volunteer bias and personality traits in sexual standards research'. *Archives of Sexual Behav.* (4) 161–71.

Burton, F.D. (1971): 'Sexual climax in female *Macaca mulatta*'. In *Proc. 3rd Int. Congress of Primatology*, vol. 3.

Cohen, H. and Shapiro, A. (1971): 'A method for measuring sexual arousal in the female'. Paper presented to Society for Psychophysiological Research, New Orleans.

Fisher, C., Cohen, H.D., Schiava, R.C., Davis, B., Furman, B., Ward, K., Edwards, A. and Cunningham, J. (1983): 'Patterns of female sexual arousal during sleep and waking: Vaginal thermo-conductance studies'. *Archives of Sexual Behav.* (12) 97–122.

Fox., C.A. (1976): 'Orgasm and fertility'. In *Progress in Sexology* (Ed. R. Gemme), Plenum Press.

Fox, C.A., Wolff, H.S. and Baker, J.A. (1970): 'Measurement of intra-vaginal and intra-uterine pressures during human coitus by radio-telemetry'. *Journal of Reproduction and Fertility* (22) 243–51.

Geer, J. and Quartararo, J. (1976): 'Vaginal blood volume responses during masturbation'. *Archives of Sexual Behav.* (5) 403–13.

Hoon, E.F., Hoon, P.W. and Wincze, J.P. (1976): 'An inventory for the measurement of female sexual arousability: The SAI'. *Archives of Sexual Behav.* (5) 291–300.

Love, M. (1983): 'Incompatible relations'. *New Scientist* issue 6 October, p. 41.

McLean et al (1983): 'Unusual side-effects of Clomipramine associated with yawning'. *Canadian Journal of Psychiatry* (November).

Newcomer, S. and Udry, R.J. (1988): 'Adolescents' honesty in a survey of sexual behaviour'. *J. Adolescent Research* (3) 419–23.

Winer, G.A., Makowski, D., Alpert, Rabbi H. and Collins, Father J. (1988): 'An analysis of experimenter effects on responses to a sex questionnaire'. *Archives of Sexual Behav.* (17) 257–63.

Wolchik, M.A., Spencer, S.L. and Lisi, I.S. (1983): 'Volunteer bias in research employing vaginal measures of sexual arousal'. *Archives of Sexual Behav.* (5).

Zumpe, D. and Michael, R.P. (1968): 'The clutching reaction and orgasm in the female rhesus monkey (*Macaca mulatta*)'. *J. Endocrinol.* (40) 117–23.

3

Matters Arising

Before committing oneself to a sexual encounter, the organized participant will want to fit it in with his or her other plans for the day. In order to make adequate scheduling arrangements, it is desirable to know just how long it will take. As we shall see, there are considerable methodological difficulties for the dedicated sex researcher in finding out just how long an average sexual encounter takes.

The crucial parameter here is known as *orgasm latency*, which is defined (following Levitt, 1983) as follows:

> *Orgasm latency is the time interval between the beginning of a directly stimulating sexual activity intended eventually to produce an orgasm – such as intromission of the penis in coitus – and the occurrence of the orgasm itself.*

In business parlance, it is the time between matters arising and any other business.

But as Levitt points out, estimates of male orgasm latency are hypothetically subject to retrospective distortion. Indeed the frequently heard post-orgasmic cry of the male – 'My goodness is that the time I really must be going'* – attests to such distortion even immediately retrospectively. How time does indeed fly when you are enjoying yourself.

*To which the conventional riposte is: 'But you've only just come.'

There is also the question of deliberate distortion, having the result of lengthening measures of orgasm latency, if subjects are merely asked how long their average encounter lasts.

To get round these problems, Levitt adopted an ingenious experimental design. Groups of medical students were shown a film in which a couple engaged in a continuous session of foreplay followed by intercourse.

After watching the film, half of them were asked to estimate how long the foreplay had lasted, and how long the intercourse had gone on. The other half were asked to judge whether the periods of foreplay and intercourse were of longer, shorter or average time for people of their own age group.

While the subjects tended to estimate correctly the time spent on foreplay, they tended to overestimate the time taken once intercourse had begun. Estimates of female subjects were, on both sections, consistently longer than those of males.

Nearly half the group thought that the time spent on foreplay was about average; over 60 per cent thought the coital period was about average. Less than 23 per cent thought that the coital period was below average.

Married couples among the subjects, showed a greater tendency to regard both time periods as above average, as compared to single subjects.

What conclusions can be drawn from all this? Sadly, very few. Women seem to think that time drags while they are watching pornographic movies. Men lose their sense of time while watching coitus, but not foreplay. Once married, people don't expect sex to take so long.

Perhaps the conclusion is that one gets quicker with practice, though Levitt's estimate would seem to leave little room for speeding things up: *'A possible inference from this investigation is that the mean young adult male orgasm latency is in the range of 2–3 minutes.'*

Some mean young adults would no doubt contest this figure. If it is wildly off the mark, the reason could be, perhaps, that the division between foreplay and coitus is too simplistic. Much research has been done to produce a considerable refinement of these two all-embracing categories, leading to a definitive agenda for the sexual meeting.

Bentler (1968 a & b) made a good start with a 21-item checklist called the Heterosexual Behaviour Hierarchy. His idea was to produce a numbered list of possible items of sexual behaviour, from number 1, 'One-minute continuous lip kissing', to number 21, 'Mutual oral manipulation of genitals to mutual orgasm'*, with the property that anyone who had indulged in any particular item might reasonably be expected also to have done all those below it in the list.

So if you have indulged in number 13: 'Oral contact with male genitals', you will probably also have tried number 10: 'Manual manipulation of female genitals to massive secretions, by male'; and if you have done number 10, you will almost certainly have enjoyed 'Kissing nipples of female breast by male', which clocks in at number 5.

One-minute continuous lip kissing

Jemail and Geer (1976) extended Bentler's list to 25 items, and extended his concept to develop a theory of sexual scripts. The notion is that 'There are conventionalized patterns of culturally shared sequences of behaviors facilitating the "doing" of sex.' In other

*It is very confusing that, in popular parlance, this is frequently referred to as '69', which appears to relate to a numbering system distinct from Bentler's hierarchy and possessing, by implication, at least 48 more items, as yet unspecified in the literature.

words, we all have similar sexual scripts, which give us a sequence of behaviour to follow which the partner expects to happen in the same order.

Jemail and Geer accordingly gave each of their experimental subjects (45 female and 78 male) the list of 25 bits of sexual behaviour, all juiced up a little by putting them into a narrative form. The subjects were asked to rearrange the sentences in an order that reflected how sexually arousing they found each passage to be.

After doing this, they were then asked to make a new arrangement to reflect how likely they thought each one was to happen in a sexual encounter. Here are the 25 sentences:

1 They shared a slow kiss, moving their tongues in and out of each other's mouths.
2 Taking his hand, she made him squeeze her firm, excited breast.
3 Roughly stroking his genitals, she made them bulge with a hard-on.
4 He slid down and began kissing her full breast, bitting [sic] each nipple.
5 Snuggling together, their bodies created more warmth.
6 Gently, he guided her hand to caress his balls.
7 His nipples erected as she sucked them gently.
8 She massaged his hard penis rhythmically.
9 He fingered her clitoris, feeling her thick, dark hair as she stroked his pulsating cock.
10 He pressed his groin against her, feeling the warmth of her genitals.
11 His hard-on swelled, pulsating with pleasure.
12 When he gently rubbed her swollen lips, she moaned with delight.
13 Her vagina felt warm as she rubbed her clitoris against him.
14 She felt a warm throbbing in her genitals.
15 As his finger played inside her wet lips, she began to moan.
16 Using his tongue, he licked her clitoris, moving her lips

He pressed his groin against her, feeling the warmth of her genitals

apart gently yet firmly.

17 She began to cover his peter [sic] with kisses.

18 While he thrust his tongue deep in her vagina, she sucked his hardened penis.

19 As she forced his hard-on deeper in her mouth, she caressed him.

20 Quickly running his tongue over her wet vagina he felt her subtle quivering.

21 On top of her, he thrust deeper into her vagina, enjoying the tightness of her.

22 By raising her hips, she enjoyed the full length of his tool.

23 Throbbing, his member exploded into orgasm.

24 Their surging orgasm triggered a pulsing in their genitals.

25 Her hot vagina exploded into her own orgasm.

What was most interesting about the findings were the differences caused by the various conditions of arrangement: male, arousal and likely, and female, arousal and likely.

Pooling the data from the respondents, the following tables emerged indicating the estimated ranking of the above items:

male arousing:	1 2 3 4 5 6 7 8 9 10 11 12 13 14 15 16 17 18 19 20 21 22 23 24 25
male likely:	1 2 4 5 7 3 6 10 8 9 15 13 12 11 17 16 14 20 18 19 21 22 24 25 23

female arousing: 1 2 4 6 7 5 10 3 9 14 15 8 11 13 16 12 20 17 18 19 21 22 25 23 24
female likely: 1 2 4 5 6 10 7 9 8 15 3 14 13 12 11 16 17 20 18 19 21 25 22 23 24

The inconsistencies among these patterns reveal some potential areas of conflict and misunderstanding in sexual relations. For example, whereas men find that *roughly stroking his genitals, she made them bulge with a hard-on* (number 3) is hardly arousing at all, and yet expect it to happen only after *his nipples erected as she sucked them gently* (7), women find the same bulge-inducing rough-stroking even more exciting than *he pressed his groin against her, feeling the warmth of her genitals* (10), and she is not likely to do it until just after *his finger played inside her wet lips and she began to moan* (15).

Equally revealing were the items which subjects chose not to include in their lists. When arranging the sentences, they were permitted to discard sentences that they thought unarousing or unlikely.

More than a third of both male and female respondents discarded the sentence describing the female kissing the male's nipples, under both 'arousing' and 'likely' conditions. The researchers put this down to socio-cultural influences on the script since 'conventionally the man's nipples are not defined as erogenous'.

Females discarded more items in their 'likely to occur' list than they did under 'arousing', which seems to imply a rather pessimistic viewpoint. In particular, *while he thrust his tongue deep in her vagina, she sucked his hardened penis* was discarded by 51 per cent of women in their 'likely to occur' list, but dropped by only 27 per cent in their arousing sequences.

On the other hand, or to be more accurate, mouth, 35 per cent of males (and only 8 per cent of females) discarded *he slid down and began kissing her full breast, bitting* [sic] *each nipple* in the 'arousing' list, though only 8 per cent (both males and females) thought it unlikely to happen. So there is general agreement that men are likely to do a bit of nipple-nibbling, though more than one in three men do not find it arousing.

The authors speculate that 'males engage in this behaviour mainly to fulfil the conventional expectation that this is arousing to females'.

Generally, however, there is a strong measure of agreement between males and females in their choice of discarded items. Apart from the above item, only three other items showed significant sex-differences in the piles of discards:

Females tended to discard *she began to cover his peter with kisses* (both as likely and arousing) more than males. It is implied that the use of the word 'peter' may have contributed to this difference. Regrettably, separate figures on this item for men named Peter are not available.

Males tended to discard *she felt a warm throbbing in her genitals* (both conditions) and *throbbing, his member exploded into orgasm* (arousal only). It is suggested that throbbing is something that is done primarily by women.

The researchers finally conclude:

> In general these results support the notion inherent in sexual scripting theory that the sexes have a mutually shared conventionalized sequence which plots the behaviors in a heterosexual interaction and agrees in what is defined as sexually arousing.

It is possible, however, to go further and speculate on what this research tells us about the true likely progression of such a heterosexual interaction. Since both participants will be following their 'likely' lists, we can be sure that it will start with numbers 1, 2, 4 and 5 (agreed by both male and female), when we reach a brief impasse as the female waits for him to guide her hand to caress his balls, while his is waiting for her to suck his nipples. He will also wait in vain for her to stroke his genitals roughly, before getting back on course with 6 and guiding her hand to caress his balls.

They both agree that what happens next is 10 (groin-pressing and feeling genital warmth), but he will be disappointed to find that she then sucks his nipples instead of massaging his hard penis rhythmically. Having given up on that, he will probably move ahead to a spot of clitoris fingering (9) when she'll get the message and stroke his pulsating cock.

The trouble then is that if by now, as is highly probable, he has an erection, she will think they are back at number three, will proceed to her next item, 14, which drives him on to 20, when they rush headlong (or at least tonguelong) into 18 and 19, turn round for 21 and then her hot vagina explodes into her own orgasm just when he's expecting her to raise her hips and enjoy the full length of his tool.

The whole procedure seems full of potential misunderstandings and would seem to require a good deal of rehearsal if anyone is ever to get it right. Though you can

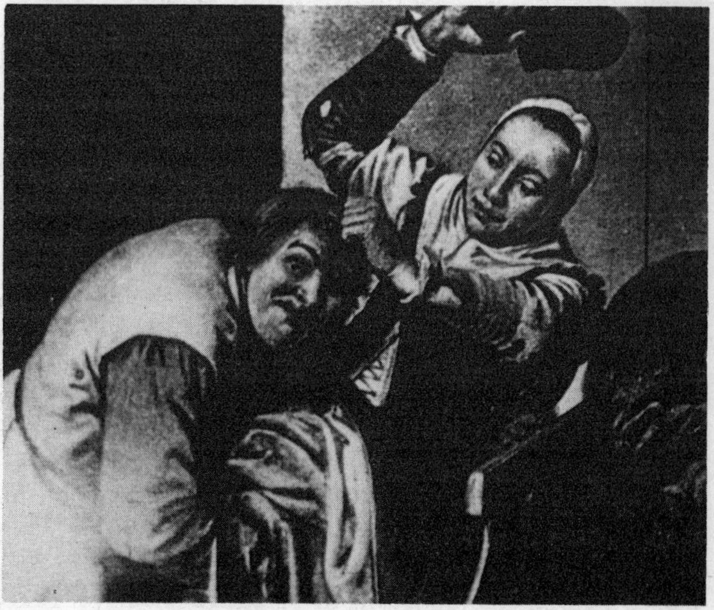

The whole procedure seems full of potential misunderstandings

Subjects masturbated to orgasm while attached to electroencephalographs

understand how, with the script not yet agreed, they can be rushed from 21 to 23 in under three minutes.

When things do go wrong, what is most likely, according to Maass and Volpato (1989) is that the male will blame the female. In two studies (with 84 females and 81 males) the subjects were asked to describe and explain both satisfying and unsatisfying sexual experiences in their past, ascribing a cause to things that went wrong.

The study showed that men's attributions tended to be self-serving, tending to assign responsibility for failure to the partner, while women's explanations were generally more self-derogatory.

The other thing any thinking person will want to know before rushing ahead with sex is what effect it will have on his or her brain. This was answered by Cohen, Rosen and Goldstein (1976) in a series of experiments with subjects who masturbated to orgasm while attached to electro-encephalographs.

The subjects were four males and three females. One of the males was homosexual; one of the females was left-handed; and they all masturbated at least twice a week. During the experiments, three of the females and one of the males used an electric vibrator, the others used their hands. Two of the subjects were shown erotic films to help things along by enhancing sexual fantasy.

Each subject manually masturbated until one or more satisfactory orgasms had been attained. In order to signal orgasm, the subject was instructed to depress a switch at the onset of the climax and to release the switch as soon as the orgasm was completed.

What the EEG readings identified were considerable changes in the right/left amplitude ratios, indicating marked changes in the relative nature of right-brain and left-brain activity during orgasm. Except for the left-handed subject, there was a large increase in the amplitudes of the right hemisphere, accompanied by much smaller increases in amplitude in the left hemisphere.

But was this directly due to orgasm, or might it have been in some way connected to the choice of masturbating hand? In order to settle the matter, they invited two of the subjects back to masturbate with the other hand. The male, though evidently unused to it, masturbated successfully left-handed, and produced the same EEG effect.

The woman, who was the exclusively left-hander, found another way to satisfy the experimenters, which was to fake an orgasm while simulating all the movements of her normal left-handed masturbation. The EEG effect disappeared, thus indicating that it must have been caused by the orgasm.

The interpretation of what these brain wave patterns mean is difficult, since 'It is a qualitatively different kind of interhemispheric change unrelated to other changes described so far in the scientific literature.'

But it does provide a valid way of testing for faked orgasms.

This is also believed to be the only instance in scientific or non-scientific literature of a faked orgasm during masturbation.

References and further reading

Bentler, P.M. (1968a): 'Heterosexual Behaviour Assessment: 1. Males'. *Behav. Res. Ther.* (6) 21–25.

Bentler, P.M. (1968b): 'Heterosexual Behaviour Assessment: 2. Females'. *Behav. Res. Ther.* (6) 27–30.

Cohen, H.D., Rosen, R.C. and Goldstein, L. (1976): 'Electroencephalographic laterality changes during human sexual orgasm'. *Archives of Sexual Behav.* (5) 189–99.

Jemail, J.J. and Geer, J. (1976): 'Sexual Scripts'. In *Progress in Sexology* (Ed. R. Gemme), Plenum Press.

Levitt, E.E. (1983): 'Estimating the duration of sexual behaviour: A laboratory analog study'. *Archives of Sexual Behav.* (12).

Maass, A. and Volpato, C. (1989): 'Gender differences in self-serving attributions about sexual experiences'. *J. App. Social Psychology* (19) 517–42.

4

Onwards and Upwards

Once the penile tumescence gauge became accepted as standard laboratory equipment, it began to be used in a range of experiments to measure more sophisticated and increasingly imaginative aspects of men's reactions to erotic stimuli.

Hale and Strassberg (1990) investigated the depressing effect that anxiety can have on a man's potency. In their experiment, 54 men watched erotic videos after being prepared in one of three different ways.

Group One were given no information but just allowed to watch while their reactions were monitored; group Two were told that while watching the film, they were liable to receive mild electric shocks; group Three were told that their baseline level of sexual arousal was subnormal.

The readings on the tumescence gauge showed that conditions two and three interfered substantially with sexual arousal.

Much of the early work with the penile tumescence gauge was designed to demonstrate that subjective arousal correlated with physiological arousal. Bancroft (1971) found that at very low levels of physiological arousal, the subject is liable not to notice that he is aroused at all. Later, other researchers, notably Farkas, Sine and Evans (1979) confirmed that, in general, subjective assessments of arousal correlated better with tumescence gauge readings at higher levels of tumescence.

But what is the best way to get aroused? Is it enough to think dirty and if so what precisely should you think about? Or is it better to watch a dirty movie? These themes and more were investigated in great statistical detail by Smith and Over (1987).

They started by building on a good deal of earlier research which had demonstrated that Masters and Johnson were quite wrong when they said: 'No man can wish, will or demand an erection' and 'Attainment of an erection is something over which he has absolutely no voluntary control.' Rubin and Henson (1975) were among those who showed that exactly the opposite may be the case.

So Smith and Over had their 66 male subjects attempt to gain erection by indulging in fantasy. They measured their circumferential indications of success with penile tumescence gauges, asked them for subjective assessments of arousal, and asked them to give details of the fantasies.

Later they repeated the procedure with the same men watching a dirty film ('depicting heterosexual interaction') instead of fantasizing.

The subjects ranged in age from eighteen to thirty-three (median twenty-one years); three of them admitted to being virgins; 42 of them said they had a current sexual partner. They reported a mean frequency of 5.12 orgasms a week, of which 2.78 were derived from heterosexual activity, 3.20 from masturbation, and 0.12 from wet dreams.

After filling in various questionnaires relating to personality, sexual experience and visual imagery, each subject sat ('semisupine in a comfortable recliner chair') for the 90-minute test session. He was instructed in how to put on the penile tumescence gauge and told, once it was on, not to touch his penis. After a period of relaxation to obtain baseline measurements on the gauge, he was asked to reach as high a level of sexual arousal as possible by engaging in sexual fantasy for two minutes. This was repeated over six two-minute sessions, with 30 seconds relaxation between

How to put on the penile tumescence gauge: The Wrong Way

each of them.

At the end of the sixth session, the subject was asked to rate the level of subjective arousal he had reached on an 11-point scale where 1 corresponds to 'not sexually exciting', 6 is 'moderately exciting', and 11 is 'wildly sexually exciting'. After that, he had to complete the Sexual Fantasy Questionnaire.

The final part of the testing involved the subject watching a six-minute video 'which depicted a man and woman undressing and then engaging in manual genital fondling, fellatio, cunnilingus and intercourse'.

Again the subject had to rate his level of subjective arousal.

The wide range of differences in individuals' penile circumference changes during the fantasy sessions (expansion varied from 1 mm to 41 mm with a mean change of 13.85 mm) suggested that some subjects were much better at fantasizing than others.

Youth and masturbation frequency seemed to lead to increased fantasy-induced tumescence, but other personality variables seemed to have little importance, so the researchers turned their attention to the content of the fantasies.

'The question of interest is whether subjects who differed in the extent to which they could achieve erection through fantasy employed different sexual themes when engaging in fantasy.' In other words, do some fantasies lead to better erections than others?

Accordingly, they listed all the various components of people's fantasies, ending up with 42 sexual activity themes, and correlated the occurrence of the themes with each other and with arousal measures.

> Erotic value scores for the 42 themes were subjected to factor analysis in order to identify fantasy content dimensions. After ten principal components with eigenvalues greater than unity had been found, rotation of the matrix using the Oblimin procedure yielded an optimal solution of five factors, which collectively accounted for 64 per cent of variance.

Pretty wild!

What this all means, is that a statistical analysis identifies the five main factors out of which all sexual fantasies are made. They are:

- Sex in Public (including sexual activity with many women at the same time)
- Sexual Aggression (including humiliating a woman)
- Sensual Activity (including breast-stroke and nipple-nibbling)
- Genital-related Activity (the favourite was oral stimulation of a woman's genitals)
- Dominance–Submission (usually with the man tied up and/or raped by a woman)

Scores on these five fantasy factors were then correlated

with scores on the penile tumescence gauge to see which factors were associated with the best erections. What showed most strongly was that genital-related fantasies had the highest correlation with penile tumescence.

Whether this result is any use to anyone is a matter for conjecture. It could be that genital-related fantasies are the best buy in the erection department, or it could be that men who are better at achieving erection through fantasy are more likely to indulge in genital-related fantasies. To what extent is the erection the product of the fantasy, and how much is the fantasy affected by the erection?

Clearly further research is badly needed on this elusive matter.

When they moved over to watching the dirty film, however, the results became still less clear. The film was clearly more arousing than fantasy, both subjectively (averaging 7.58 on the 11-point scale compared with 4.66) and tumescently (penile circumferences expanding by an average of 20.69 mm compared with 13.86 mm), but there was little information on who had the best erections and why.

The best result was a strong negative correlation between age and subjective arousal, which may be taken either to suggest that dirty old men enjoy pornographic films less than dirty young men, or that dirty old men have more highly developed tastes in the matter, and are consequently more difficult to impress.

But there are more ways to strain a tumescence gauge than fantasizing or watching blue movies. In Julien and Over (1988) the experimenters set about the task of comparing arousal levels obtained by watching films, looking at photographs, listening to spoken text, reading written text and fantasizing.

Before they came along, a good deal of earlier research had left conflicting and confused results. While most experiments found that film was more potent than pictures, and generally that explicit stimuli are more effective than less explicit erotica, Tannenbaum (1970) showed that rape scenes in film are less arousing when portrayed than when their occurrence is merely implied. Also Campagna (1976) found that self-generated fantasies were in general more arousing than erotic stories.

What was less than convincing about much of the early work was that insufficient was done to equate the content of the erotic material across the different modes of presentation. So for their study, Julien and Over made a film of heterosexual interaction but also took still photographs from the same angles as the film camera, and wrote a text describing the events portrayed in the film. Finally, they prepared a list of phrases describing the sexual activities portrayed in the film in the order they happened.

They thus had the means to provide erotic stimulation, using the same story-line across five different modes of presentation:

1 Subjects watch it on video
2 Subjects follow it through a series of snapshots
3 The story is read to them
4 They read the story themselves
5 They indulge in a guided fantasy, following the phrases provided

'The question of interest was whether sexual arousal differed systematically across these five modes of stimulation.'

Each of the 24 male, heterosexual, sexually active volunteers (aged eighteen to fifty-two, median age twenty-six) was fitted with a mercury-in-silicon rubber strain gauge to measure penile tumescence while they sat through five 45-minute stimulating sessions. Baseline levels were established by a preliminary period of relaxing music and pictures of ducks swimming or walking but not doing anything rude by a river bank. With at least a day's rest between sessions, all subjects eventually sampled each of the five modes of presentation described above.

The material within each mode was divided into eight 2-minute segments: 1) a man and a woman undressing each other; 2) mutual fondling; 3) mutual masturbation; 4) cunnilingus; 5) mutual oral sex; 6) fellatio; 7) intercourse in several positions; and 8) intercourse terminating in ejaculation. Between each segment there was a 30-second interval without stimulation.

For the photographs, each segment was represented by four pictures, each displayed for 30 seconds; for the spoken text, the story was read by a young woman who used volume, pitch and pauses to match the level of activity on the video.

Every twenty seconds, a record was taken of the penile tumescence level, and the subject had to put a cross on a line representing his subjective assessment of arousal. One end of the line was marked 'not sexually exciting', the other end 'wildly sexually exciting', with 'moderately sexually exciting' in the middle.

The results, both on subjective assessment and penile engorgement, showed that all methods of arousal achieved moderate success during the first two-minute segment (undressing), rose sharply during the second (fondling), then climbed until peaking at segment six (fellatio) before beginning a gradual decline in the final two segments towards ejaculation.

Comparing the results of different methods of arousal showed film to be by far the best, followed by spoken text, photographs, written text and fantasy in that order. The order of film, spoken text, written text and fantasy is perfectly consistent throughout all eight segments, with the most anomalous results being produced by photographs, where the arousal level falls below written text for segment 3 (mutual masturbation), regains its normal position for cunnilingus and mutual oral sex, and then overtakes spoken text for fellatio before falling behind both spoken and written text for intercourse in several positions and ejaculation.

In their discussion of these results, the researchers state:

> If it can be assumed that there was equivalence in content at the level where reliable translation from one mode to another could have been accomplished, the conclusion must be that film was the most arousing of the five modes because of factors unique to film.

They do, however, cast some doubt on even this tentative conclusion, because they started with the film, then tried to make the other modes of stimulation match it. 'Possibly the text proved to be less arousing than the film because the translation undertaken in the present study was inaccurate or not comprehensive enough.'

Clearly a great deal more research is needed before we can be quite sure that dirty films really are as dirty as we think.

We cannot leave the important topic of effect of erotica on erections, without considering social pressures. Particularly in a laboratory setting, or when experiencing sexual stimulation in the presence of another person, everyone is liable to be conscious of certain social expectations. And knowledge of those expectations can affect performance.

Coyne and Cross (1988) investigated this aspect by the simple expedient of letting men know what the readings were on other men's penile tumescence gauges. More accurately, their subjects thought that they were being told the readings on another man's gauge, though in fact they were being fed with bogus data carefully controlled by the experimenters.

Their ingredients for this experiment included the following:

- 2 Parks Type A strain gauges
- cable connectors
- 1 Parks Model 240 Plethysmograph
- 2 Wavetek Model 114 Voltage Control Generators (VCG)
- 1 Beckman Type R Dynograph
- Assorted videotapes (2 minutes each) depicting female nudes

- Assorted videotapes (3 minutes each) depicting fellatio and intercourse
- 1 warm-up tape (6 minutes) of fellatio, mutual masturbation, cunnilingus and intercourse
- 2 isolated booths
- 99 volunteers

Unfortunately, of the 99 volunteers, data had to be discarded for 'nine men because of situational impotence, for one man because he correctly suspected the experimental manipulations, and for one because he was both impotent and suspicious'.

So the remaining 88 men were put into pairs for the experiment. They were told that they were going to watch non-deviant heterosexual videos, and that they would be able to *hear* the effects the video was having on their partner.

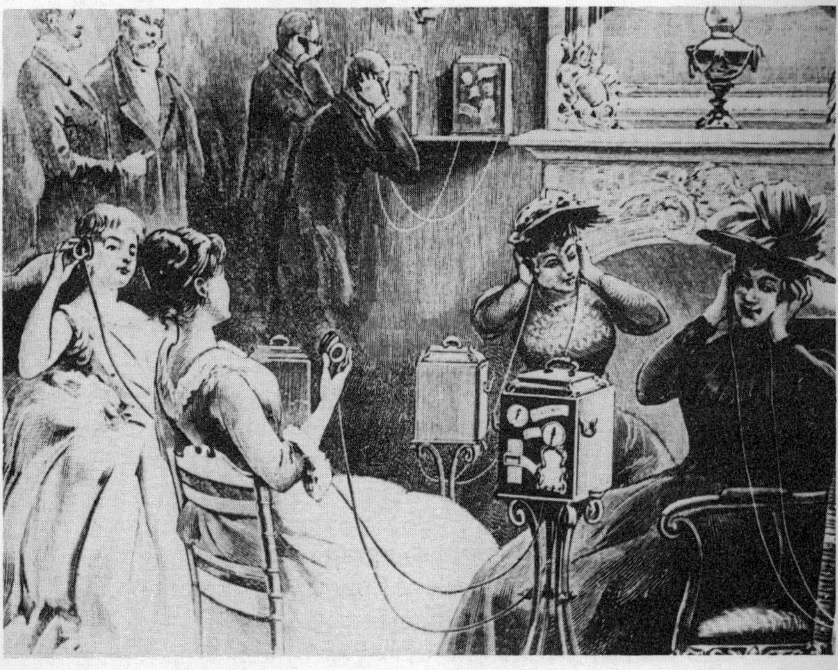

They would be able to hear the effects the video was having on their partner

By feeding the tumescence gauge signal through the VCG, a sound could be produced that became progressively higher in pitch as arousal increased.

What they in fact heard was not the sound of their partner's erections, but one of three standard response patterns:

1 Low Model – consisting of a low hum varying only slightly in pitch throughout the session (corresponding to at most only slight stimulation).
2 High Model – consisting of a tone quickly rising to high pitch, then staying at a high level throughout.
3 No Model – hearing feedback of their own erection.

So in High Model state, they think their partner is highly aroused, in Low Model, they think he is not excited at all, and in No Model, they think his reaction is identical to their own.

The other variable that the experimenters decided to manipulate was the subjects' expectations of the effects of being able to hear their partner's erections straining away at their gauges. So they told some of the subjects that being able to hear their partner tended to increase a man's erections and they told others that it would decrease their erections. Those in the No Model group above were given no such advice at all.

So we have 88 men watching videos in pairs, some watching nudes, some watching intercourse, some believing their partners are getting very aroused, some thinking their partners are totally unaroused, some thinking they ought to be getting more aroused themselves and some thinking they should be getting less aroused. Others did not know whether they should be getting aroused at all, and were listening to their own penis thinking it was someone else's.

Meanwhile, the plethysmograph was twitching its pens to match every movement of their penises, and the results for each man were converted to percentages of full erection.

After every session, each subject was asked to estimate:

a) how high he thought his erection reached; b) how attractive (for nudes) or exciting (for intercourse) he found the film, and c) how disgusting he found it.

When all the data had been gathered and correlated, among the more interesting findings were the following:

Men find nudes more attractive if they hear other men having erections while viewing them. They also find them more disgusting.

If you believe that hearing another man's erection will decrease your own, then you are likely to find pictures of nudes more disgusting, whether the sounds you hear indicate that your partner is highly aroused or not aroused at all.

Whereas self-reported erection and excitement both tend to give accurate guides to measured erection, these correlations go haywire if you think you are listening to

Men who viewed intercourse were consistently more disgusted than those who viewed nudes

someone who is not aroused at all. In fact, the confusion of listening to someone else who is not responding can make you think you are psychologically unexcited when the opposite is the case.

Reactions to videotapes are not greatly affected by listening to other men's erections. 'The ability of explicit intercourse stimuli to elicit high arousal . . . may have overwhelmed any effect of social influence to decrease the erections of men who heard feedback from an ostensibly bored co-participant.'

Men who viewed intercourse were consistently more disgusted than those who viewed nudes.

Despite a large volume of negative findings, the researchers do consider their positive results strong enough to support the conclusion that: '*For some men, attractive women are such sufficiently ambiguous stimuli that both erections and perceptions can be influenced by another man's reactions.*'

References and further reading

Arndt, W.B., Foehl, J.C. and Good, F.E. (1985): 'Specific sexual fantasy themes: A multidimensional study'. *J. Pers. Soc. Psychol.* (48) 472–8.

Bancroft, J. (1971): 'The application of psychophysiological measures to the assessment and modification of sexual behaviour'. *Behaviour Res. and Ther.* (9) 119–30.

Campagna, (1976): 'Normative and functional aspects of young men's masturbation fantasies'. Unpublished Ph.D. dissertation, Yale Univ.

Coyne, B.J. and Cross, H.J. (1988): 'Effects of social pressure on erections and evaluations of erotica'. *J. Sex Research* (25) 397–411.

Farkas, G.M., Sine, L.F. and Evans, I.M. (1979): 'The effects of distraction, performance demand, stimulus explicitness and personality on objective and subjective measures of sexual arousal'. *Behav. Res. and Ther.* (17) 25–32.

Hale, V.E. and Strassberg, D.S. (1990): 'The role of anxiety on sexual arousal'. *Archives of Sexual Behav.* (19) 569–81.

Julien, E. and Over, R. (1988): 'Male sexual arousal across five modes of erotic stimulation'. *Archives of Sexual Behav.* (17) 131–43.

Rosen, R.C. (1973): 'Suppression of penile tumescence by instrumental conditioning'. *Psychosom. Med.* (35) 509–14.

Rubin, H.B. and Henson, D.E. (1975): 'Voluntary enhancement of penile erection'. *Bull. Psychon. Soc.* (38) 666–73.

Smith, D. and Over, R. (1987): 'Correlates of fantasy-induced and film-induced male sexual arousal'. *Archives of Sexual Behav.* (16) 395–409.

Tannenbaum, P.A. (1970): 'Emotional arousal as a mediator of communication effects'. In Technical Reports of the Commission on Obscenity and Pornography, vol. 8. US Govt Printing Office, Washington DC.

5

The Quest for the Holy G-Spot

Ever since Grafenberg's lone sighting (Grafenberg, 1950) of the fabled spot that bears his name, the existence of this mythical place has been a subject of deep contention. The team of Addiego, Belzer, Comolli, Moger, Perry and Whipple found it in 1981, and Perry and Whipple returned later the following year, then mounted another expedition in 1982.

In 1983, Goldberg, Whipple, Fishkin, Waxman, Fink and Weisberg looked even more closely into the matter and announced their belief in the existence of a clearly defined erogenous zone, called the Grafenberg or G-spot, on the anterior vaginal wall, the stimulation of which provokes orgasm.

Yet the dispute continues. Some still cling to the belief that only stimulation of the clitoris can produce orgasm. Others believe that vaginal stimulation on its own is sufficient, even without the existence of a G-spot.

The issue might, perhaps, be shrugged off as unimportant. After all, one might say, an orgasm is good news wherever it comes from. But that would be to ignore a point of major historical weight: the question of whether E. Grafenberg should become the first man to have a part of the female anatomy named after him since the sixteenth-century Italian anatomist Fallopius bought his season ticket to eternity on the tubes.

Grafenberg establishes base camp on the slopes of Mons Veneris

No man has expended greater energy in searching for the truth about female orgasm than Dr Heli Alzate, Professor of Sexology at Caldas University School of Medicine in Manizales, Colombia, and we shall be quoting extensively from his researches later in this chapter.

Before proceeding with his vaginal explorations, however, it will be helpful to spend a little time around the clitoris.

Fisher (1973) made an extensive survey of women's orgasmic preferences. On a 7-point scale, ranging from exclusively vaginal to exclusively clitoral stimulation, he found that the average response fell halfway between 'I prefer a moderate amount of clitoral stimulation' and 'I prefer a considerable amount of clitoral stimulation'. Furthermore, 29 per cent of women indicated that 'clitoral stimulation contributes much more than vaginal stimulation' towards attaining orgasm and another 20 per cent agreed that 'clitoral stimulation contributes somewhat more than vaginal stimulation'. The figures for vaginal stimulation contributing much more and somewhat more were only 7 per cent and 5 per cent respectively.

Still furthermore, approximately 19 per cent of the women indicated 'I cannot attain orgasm without clitoral stimulation', while only about 3 per cent said that they preferred no clitoral stimulation at all.

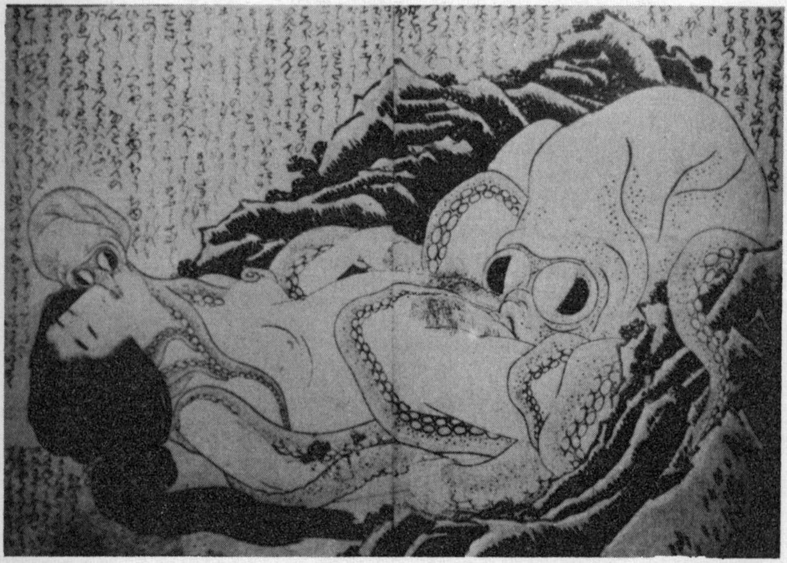

'I prefer a moderate amount of clitoral stimulation'

Yet still furthermore, given the choice between exclusive clitoral and exclusive vaginal stimulation, the clitoris wins by 64 per cent to 36 per cent.

And furthermost of all, women who preferred vaginal stimulation seemed to be more tense and emotional, and have a lower threshold for feeling disturbed than their clitoris-orientated counterparts.

Despite all this clitoral propaganda, Alzate persevered with his stimulating work on the vaginal walls in Alzate and Londoño (1984 and 1987) and Alzate (1985). It is the last of these papers that chronicles his greatest achievements.

'The purpose of this study – which was approved by the Research Committee of Caldas University – was to replicate the findings of Alzate and Londoño (1984) in the hope of reaching a better understanding of vaginal eroticism', he explains before proceeding to the section on experimental method.

> The subjects were 27 apparently healthy, coitally experienced, paid volunteers who gave informed consent and were free to stop the research procedure at any time, although none did. They were mostly (82 per cent) overt or covert prostitutes; the remainder were prostitutes' friends, apparently not active in the trade. Most of them (82 per cent)* were recruited through the good offices of a madam with whom the experimenter was acquainted, the remainder being recruited with the help of the same subjects . . . each received a fee of about $14 per examining session.

After taking down their credentials (mean age 24.1) the professor got down to business, with the subject supine on

*It is not specifically stated that these are the same 82 per cent as the 82 per cent referred to earlier, but it seems reasonable to assume so. Anyway, this book has been very short of footnotes until now and this seemed a good place to put one in.

the examining table, knees bent (unless she felt more comfortable with them extended):

> The author, with his hands washed, inserted his lubricated index and/or middle fingers into the subject's vagina and proceeded to systematically friction both vaginal walls, applying a moderate to strong rhythmic pressure at an angle to the wall, going from the lower to the upper half of the vagina, and starting at the posterior wall. The subject was asked to indicate the sensations, erotic or other, she was experiencing in the different stimulated zones, and when a region of increasing erotic sensitivity was found, increasingly stronger pressure was applied until either the subject reached orgasm or the examiner's fatigue made him stop stimulation. In order to record more precisely some subjects' responses, a second examination was conducted on several subjects.

The score-board at the end read as follows:

> All 27 subjects reported vaginal erotic sensitivity on one or both walls.
> 85 per cent were sensitive on the posterior wall (mostly on the lower half).
> 74 per cent were sensitive on the anterior wall (always on the upper half, but in 60 per cent of subjects on the lower half as well).
> 24 of the 27 subjects reached orgasm.
> 92 per cent of those who reached orgasm climaxed twice or more.
> One had eight orgasms.
> The average time to reach orgasm was between 3 and 4 minutes.

On these last points, the professor states that 'It appears that the limiting factors for the majority of women not having many consecutive climaxes were experimenter's or subject's fatigue and time constraints.'

There was also the matter of orgasmic ejaculation to investigate. Although nine of the subjects reported the impression of having expelled a fluid, this was impossible to confirm. There was a suggestion that such emissions were confused with either vaginal lubrication or urinary incontinence caused by the stress of orgasm.

A further experiment was performed on one subject who emphatically maintained that she often ejaculated at orgasm:

> After having established that she had no urge to urinate, she was invited to stimulate her clitoris to orgasm while the experimenter, with his fingers motionless inside her vagina, observed. At orgasm a fluid that spilled over the experimenter's hand was effectively expelled through the subject's urethra in an estimated amount of 5–10 ml . . . At another session, samples of both the subject's urine and her orgasmic emission were collected for chemical analysis. Results showed that the orgasmic emission was chemically indistinguishable from her urine sample.

'The subject's urine and her orgasmic emission were collected for chemical analysis'

Although expressing caution about generalizing the results of this 'opportunistic' sample to the general female population, and expressing concern about the possible effect of interplay between experimenter and subject on the latter's arousal, one strong conclusion is reached from this series of experiments: *'This study's findings do not support the existence of the discrete anatomical structure called the Grafenberg spot.'*

The author's concluding paragraph begins with the

words 'Some comments on the ethical implication of this research, which may be a cause of concern, are in order.' Following the lead of Masters and Johnson, he contends that 'As long as the experimenter does not become erotically involved with the subject, this or a similar research procedure is ethically acceptable.'

If there were still any critics of his experimental procedures, he silenced them in Alzate and Londoño (1987), which was a follow-up to Alzate and Londoño (1984).

In the 1987 paper, the experimenters contacted the 24 female subjects of their original research on vaginal erotic sensitivity and asked them for retrospective reactions. The results indicated that the subjects experienced little or no discomfort during the experiment and no negative after-effects. 'In fact, many subjects found their participation personally rewarding.'

Of the non-prostitutes participating in that study, 79.2 per cent had become sexually aroused; and 91.7 per cent of the total sample said they would be willing to do it again.

Most reassuring of all, only one subject thought that the male experimenter became sexually aroused during the experiment, and none at all thought that the female experimenter had become aroused.

Returning to the G-spot, there was an analogous experiment in Czechoslovakia reported in Zaviacic, Zaviacicova, Holoman and Molcan (1988), where 27 patients who were being treated for infertility volunteered to be stimulated to see if urethral expulsions could be induced.

> Stimulation was performed at the out-patient department once or twice a week, usually in the afternoons or early evening hours. Over the course of the four sessions, stimulation was administered to each woman by both the female and male members of our medical research team (one woman and three men). Minimally, two members of our team were always present during a stimulatory session.

The stimulation took the form of 'digital palpation of the anterior wall of the vagina, using one or two fingers'. The technique apparently differed from that of Prof. Alzate in that the Czechoslovakian experimenters wore surgical gloves.

Although all the subjects had emptied their bladders before the procedure, they tended to feel a growing need to urinate as arousal increased. When urethral expulsions occurred, the outflowing liquid was collected in a porcelain vessel.

> In some women stimulations were repeated immediately after the first procedure. The reason for repeating the stimulation in one of the women in the 'easily induced expulsions group' was her exceptional responsiveness . . . Five consecutive stimulations yielded up to 16 ml of ejaculate.

The results of the experiment led to a classification of the subjects into four categories:

Non-ejaculators (n=17) who were excused from further testing after four sessions had produced no ejaculate.

The relatively hard-to-induce expulsions group (n=3) 'Characterized by great personal involvement in the stimulation and considerable demands on vaginal digital friction and duration.'

The easily induced expulsions group (n=2) for whom 'The release of the fluid from the urethra occurred after a very short time (maximally 1.5 minutes) of G-spot stimulation. Neither during stimulation nor ejaculation was any other visual manifestation of sexual arousal observed in these two women.' One of them was a 37-year-old 'in whom over 160 stimulations resulted in ejaculation'.

The intermediate group (n=5) for whom around five minutes of stimulation was required, but far less intensive than in the hard-to-induce group.

The researchers try to relate these categories to earlier attempts to classify orgasmic patterns in women, but end

Disinfecting the examination area after the experiment

by saying: 'Our suggestions concerning typology of the female ejaculators are limited due to the small size of our series. Further investigations are required to confirm the suggested typology.'

They are, however, sure of one thing: '*A specifically sensitive site (the G-spot) was located in all 27 women in which a manually detectable tumescence developed at the location of the sensitive site.*'

Finally, if anyone should be contemplating a visit to the Columbian brothels where Prof. Alzate recruited so many of his experimental subjects, they should first read De Gallo and Alzate (1976) which corrects several commonly held misconceptions about prostitution. Their findings were based on interviews with 62 prostitutes held in December

1969 and January 1970. Among their results were the following:

- 100 per cent of the prostitutes in the survey were Catholics.
- 50 per cent attended mass regularly.
- 76 per cent went into prostitution for pressing financial reasons.
- 79 per cent 'served' two or three clients a night.
- 13 per cent had coitus with four or more customers a night.
- The average fee was fifty pesos ($2.50).
- They all performed only 'straight' sexual acts.
- 74 per cent reached orgasm during commercial coitus, 'provided that the girl liked the client and he used a good arousing technique'.
- Most of them tried to avoid orgasm, 'mainly because of disliking the client or the fear of pregnancy'.
- 60 per cent of male students have their first intercourse with a prostitute.

References and further reading

Alzate, H. (1985): 'Vaginal eroticism: A replication study'. *Archives of Sexual Behav.* (14) 529–37.

Alzate, H. and Hoch, Z. (1986): 'The "G spot" and "female ejaculation": A current appraisal'. *J. Sex and Marital Ther.* (12) 211–20.

Alzate, H. and Londoño, M.L. (1984): 'Vaginal erotic sensitivity'. *J. Sex and Marital Ther.* (10) 49–56.

Alzate, H. and Londoño, M.L. (1987): 'Subjects' reactions to a sexual experimental situation'. *J. Sex Research* (23) 362–7.

De Gallo, M.T. and Alzate, H. (1976): 'Brothel prostitution in Colombia'. *J. Sex Research* (5) 1–7.

Fischer, J. (1983): 'Die Ejakulation der Frau'. *Sexualmedizin* (12) 262–4.

Fisher, S. (1973): *Understanding the Female Orgasm*. Penguin Books.

Goldberg, D.C., Whipple, B., Fishkin, R.E., Waxman, H., Fink, P.J. and Weisberg, M. (1983): 'The Grafenberg spot and female ejaculation: A review of initial hypotheses'. *J. Sex and Marital Ther.* (9) 27–37.

Grafenberg, E. (1950): 'The role of urethra in female orgasm'. *Int. J. Sexol.* (3) 145–8.

Heath, D. (1984): 'An investigation into the origin of a copious vaginal discharge during intercourse: "Enough to wet the bed" – that "is not urine" '. *J. Sex Research* (20) 194–215.

Perry, J.D. and Whipple, B. (1981): 'Pelvic muscle strength of female ejaculators: Evidence in support of a new theory of orgasm'. *J. Sex Research* (17) 22–39.

Perry, J.D. and Whipple, B. (1982): 'Multiple components of the female orgasm'. In *Circumvaginal Musculature and Sexual Function* (Ed. B. Graber), Karger, Basel.

Tordjman, G. (1979) 'Nouvelles acquisitions dans l'etude des orgasmes femenins'. *Cah. Sexol. Clin.* (5) 519–27.

Whipple, B. and Komisaruk, B.R. (1985): 'Elevation of pain threshold by vaginal stimulation'. *Pain* (21) 357–67.

Whipple, B. and Komisaruk, B.R. (1988): 'Analgesia produced in women by genital self-stimulation'. *J. Sex Research* (24) 130–40.

Zaviacic, M., Zaviacicova, A., Holoman, I.K. and Molcan, J. (1988): 'Female urethral expulsions evoked by local digital stimulation of the G-spot: Differences in the response pattern'. *J. Sex Research* (24) 311–18.

6

Hardly Ever on a Tuesday

We have already seen (chapter 4) that differences in sexual scripts can lead to problems in the development of a sexual encounter with a member of the opposite sex. Yet it is generally agreed that you do need another such person involved if heterosexual activity is to be enjoyed to the full. (Though before taking a final stand on that matter, one should read chapter 8.)

What are the ways in which a heterosexual sets about finding a partner for his or her erotic encounter? What are the potential problems that may occur between them as they try to find a mutually acceptable script for the encounter? Both questions have spawned a great deal of research activity, particularly the problem of mate-selection.

We shall, however, for argument's sake, begin with the question of disagreements.

Women are expected to be reluctant to engage in sexual activity

A considerable number of research studies, including Peplau, Rubin and Hill (1977) and McCormick (1979), have demonstrated that males and females are conditioned to accept different roles in sexual encounters. Men are expected to initiate, and women are expected to be reluctant to engage in sexual activity.

Jesser (1978) and Perper and Weis (1987) discovered that women do sometimes take the initiative, but no one disputes that women have wider repertoires of strategies for avoiding sex, and men have wider repertoires of strategies for pursuing it.

Byers and Lewis (1988) reasoned that such behaviour was bound to lead to men and women finding themselves frequently in antagonistic positions, with the male partner wanting a higher level of sexual involvement than the woman. They therefore set about investigating types of disagreements and strategies adopted (whether coercive or compliant) to deal with them.

Accordingly, they enlisted the services of 74 female and 58 male undergraduates (of whom two dropped out when the nature of the experiment was explained to them and a further 11 did not complete the study). At the end of each day, over a period of four weeks, each subject indicated whether or not they had been on a date. (For the purpose of this study a date was defined as any social situation they were in with a specific member of the opposite sex.) If they had been on a date, they also had to indicate whether it had involved any sexual activity (from holding hands to intercourse) and whether the man had desired a more intimate level of sexual activity than the woman.

If such a disagreement occurred, they provided further information on the type of sexual activity they were involved in prior to the disagreement, and what level of sexual activity caused the disagreement. (Both of these were indicated on an 11-item list ranging from hugging to intercourse.)

Finally, more details were asked for concerning the nature of the relationship and both participants' behaviour subsequent to the disagreement.

The broad statistics of the findings were as follows (male and female results were very highly correlated, so the data have been pooled):

- Participants had an average of 10.5 dates within the four weeks
- 7 per cent of the participants did not date at all
- 7 per cent dated, but reported no sexual activity
- 39 per cent dated, reported sexual activity, but had no disagreements
- 73 per cent of all dates involved some form of sexual activity
- On 10 per cent of those dates, there was some disagreement with the man wanting more sex than the woman.

The locations of the disagreements were:

- 27.8 per cent in the woman's bedroom
- 22.2 per cent in another room of the woman's apartment
- 18.5 per cent in the man's bedroom
- 14.8 per cent in another room of the man's apartment
- 3.7 per cent in a friend's house
- 13.1 per cent elsewhere

Getting down to details, the final league table of causes of sexual disagreements reads as follows:

Unwanted Activity	*% of Disagreements*
Intercourse	32.1
Breast fondling and kissing	23.2
Fondling woman's genitals	17.9
Oral-genital stimulation	10.7
Necking	5.4
Anal intercourse	3.6
Kiss	3.6
Fondling man's genitals	1.8
Other	1.8

Unwanted breast fondling

On more than half the occasions, however, the couple having the argument had already indulged in the disputed activity on a previous occasion.

What happened next

The women generally responded to the unwanted advance both verbally and non-verbally. *Verbal responses were:*

An unqualified 'No!'	37.5 %
A refusal implying that such advances might be acceptable at a different time or place	30.4 %
Anger or threats	3.6 %

The non-verbal refusals divided into:

Blocking or non-performance	46.4 %
Moving away or pushing man away	28.6 %
Getting up or slapping	3.6 %

Faced with these acts of non-compliance, the men then:

Stopped without asking questions	60.7 %

Stopped and asked why or when	16.1 %
Stopped and attempted to persuade	7.1 %
Stopped and showed anger or displeasure	5.4 %
Continued unwanted advances	10.7 %

And the consequence was:

Argument resolved, acceptable sex resumed	32.7 %
Argument resolved, sexual activity stopped	30.9 %
Argument goes on, woman repeats refusal	9.1 %
Argument goes on, woman emphasizes refusal	27.3%

But whether they lived happily ever after is another matter, because 12.7 per cent of the men and 21.9 per cent of the women reported less romantic interest after the disagreement.

All this gives a reasonable picture of the likely course of lovers' tiffs, but throws little light on the serious problem of date-rape and the strategies needed to prevent sexual situations from getting out of hand when conflicts arise. Sadly, the vast majority in the above study simply behaved too reasonably.

Part of the problem could have been that the study itself interfered with the results. Participants might easily have subconsciously modified their behaviour through the knowledge that they were going to record the results at the end of each date. Another factor to be taken into consideration was that the results depended on accurate self-reporting by the participants rather than objective assessments by an outside observer.

In Byers (1988), the researcher maintained a higher level of control over the experiment by inventing hypothetical date-disagreement story-lines, and asking the subjects to role-play. A typical scene, for example, ends with the words: '. . . John begins to fondle your breasts. You do not wish to have him fondle your breasts. What do you say or do?' Male subjects were presented with scenes in which, typically, Jane would say: 'I don't want to.'*

Before doing the experiments, all the subjects completed the Rape Myth Acceptance Scale (RMA) as described in Burt (1980). This 19-item scale measures prejudices or false beliefs about rape and rape victims and provides a measure of the degree to which a respondent agrees with the statement that 'Women often mean yes when they say no'.

One important factor is still missing, which is that of sexual arousal. When role-playing, the subjects will be relaxed, whereas in real life, at least for some of the later-occurring examples of sexual disagreement, they would be liable to be sexually aroused.

To take this into account, the subjects watched a videotape before the experiment, portraying either two actors in bathing suits (low arousal) or the same actors engaging in a variety of sexual activities (high arousal).

The results did show that scores on the RMA appear to some extent to predict attitudes and strength of responses to unwanted sexual advances, and that such behaviour may also be affected by having watched an erotic movie beforehand. For example: *'In the unwanted breast fondling condition, the men who viewed the erotic film were more compliant than were the men who had viewed the neutral film.'*

So if a man starts fondling a woman's breast, and she indicates that she would like him to desist, he is more likely to acquiesce if he has watched a dirty film immediately before fondling.

This might not seem what one would expect, but other results went even further:

> Surprisingly, high RMA men [the sexual bigots] were more compliant when aroused [after watching the dirty

*Subjects were allowed a free response to the question, though it would no doubt have facilitated analysis of the data if they had been constrained to a 5-point scale. In the woman's case, this could have ranged from: 'Please, John, I'd be grateful if you would desist from fondling my breasts', at one end of the scale, to 'Getcha fuckin' hand outa there, asshole' at the other.

Two actors in bathing suits (low arousal)

movie] than when not aroused. It may be that, despite their adherence to rape supportive beliefs, viewing a film that showed consensual and enjoyable sexual activities decreased these men's desire to engage in adversarial or coercive sexual interactions.

Or it could be that potential inexactitudes may exist in the predictive value of a methodology that involves the subject filling in a questionnaire, watching a dirty film, then answering hypothetical questions while role-playing a scene from an idealized date.

We move on to the problem of mate-selection. How does John find Jane in the first place?

Well, if the first place is a college bar, it should, following the results of Strouse (1987), be a doddle. Analysing the data provided by 637 Michigan college students, the researcher found that the primary reasons for visiting college bars were as follows:

- 51 per cent went there to socialize.
- 7 per cent went to meet a sexual partner.
- 6 per cent went there to drink.

In a more detailed study of 131 females and 129 males at three different bars, it was found that although only 36.5 per cent admitted that their own reasons for going to bars were social or sexual, 57 per cent believed that these were the main reasons others went there.

'Overall, the data suggest that college students go to bars for a variety of reasons, among them to meet a heterosexual partner.'

This very important discovery becomes all the more relevant when taken in conjunction with Corcoran and Thomas (1991) who went one step further by considering the effects that imbibing alcohol can have on the social relationships that bar-life engenders.

They gave 162 male and 123 female undergraduates stories to read concerning a fictional first date in which either the male or the female might drink a couple of cocktails. The other partner might also drink cocktails, or stick to soft drinks or become slightly intoxicated. With the story left unfinished at an intriguing moment, the subjects were invited to speculate on whether sexual activity would be initiated and whether the couple would have sex together.

The results showed that no matter who drinks what, the male is perceived as more likely to initiate sexual activity. The subjects did, however, believe that sex was more likely if alcohol was consumed by one or both parties. And the more they drank the more likely they were to have sex.

This might all suggest a picture of rampant permissiveness with very little commitment, but a rather different picture emerged from a study by Lewis and Burr (1975) who attempted to discover at what stage in a relationship American students tend to have premarital intercourse. They summarized their findings as a pattern of 'coitus with commitment'.

This result came from analysing 2,453 responses to questionnaires that asked subjects to state the highest degree of intimacy they had experienced at four different levels of commitment in a relationship: first date, infrequent dating, going steady and engaged.

The figures (based on a survey carried out in 1968–9) showed that 30 per cent of males had at some time or another had sex on a first date, 33 per cent had done so during infrequent dating, 48 per cent while going steady and 59 per cent while engaged. The comparable figures for women were 2 per cent, 3 per cent, 19 per cent and 40 per cent.

Apart from showing that men were considerably more permissive than women, the gradual increase for both sexes through developing levels of a relationship seemed to refute any suggestions of a love-'em-and-leave-'em, sex without commitment, mentality. '*Sexual intercourse was positively and monotonically related to commitment.*'

Whereas earlier studies had reached the same conclusion in women's behaviour, Ehrmann (1959) had found that males were less permissive at both the beginning and end of the courtship period than they were in the intermediate stages. Why had there been a change over the next decade?

Lewis and Burr suggest that it was normative constraints (the behavioural rules of society) that were responsible for the change:

> When a male had relatively little personal commitment to a female and little investment of himself in her social reputation, normative constraints would have influenced him relatively little. However, when he was relating to a female as a possible marriage partner, he would have had more investment in her conformity to the social norms and he himself would have been more influenced by these norms. The result is that in the 1950s, his participation in coitus might have been more extensive in intermediate stages of courtship than at the advanced stages. In sum, what this suggests is that proscriptive normative definitions have not changed the monotonic aspect of the relationship in the commitment proposition [that permissiveness increases with commitment to the relationship] for females, but they may have contributed to an earlier curvilinear relationship for males.

What this all seems to imply is that the more you tell young people that nice girls don't have sex before marriage, the more it encourages young men to have sex with not-nice girls whom they aren't going to marry anyway.

Much of the foregoing might suggest, to the uncharitable reader, that all men want is sex. The question of how discriminating both males and females are in their search for a mate had some light thrown on it in Smith, Waldorf and Trembath (1990) where the writers analysed the content of over 600 personal advertisements from a singles magazine.

Since the advertisers listed desirable qualities of their hoped-for respondents, the researchers were able to develop a list of 28 categories to label the aspects they were looking for. The overall conclusion was that males wanted physical attractiveness while females wanted personal understanding.

'Males attributed greater importance to physical attractiveness and thinness than did females when selecting a date.'

One might, however, speculate that the findings were more a reflection of the personalities of the advertisers: ugly men and insecure women.

A related piece of research, Mazur (1986), investigated preferred shapes of women by looking at the vital statistics of pin-ups, fashion models and Miss America contestants and analysing how they had changed over the years.

Males wanted physical attractiveness while females wanted personal understanding

The mean bust-waist-hips measurements of Miss America contest winners in the 1920s were 32-25-35, no winner having a larger bust than hips, similar to major Hollywood stars such as Clara Bow or Gloria Swanson. In the 1930s, mean measurements of Miss Americas were 34-25-35, one winner having a larger bust than hips; major film stars were Jean Harlow, Greta Garbo and Marlene Dietrich, smallish busted women noted for their faces or legs. Miss America means in the 1940s were 35-24-35, with nearly half the winners having larger busts than hips; Hollywood had introduced 'sweater girl' Lana Turner and buxom Jane Russell. Since 1950 there has been a norm of bust-hips symmetry, at least in the Miss America winners, nearly all of whom (79 per cent as of 1982) had equal bust and hip measurements.

In more recent times, the measurements of *Playboy* magazine 'playmates' are quoted as indicative of trends in beauty. The ideal height dropped from 65 inches in 1960 to 64 inches in the late 1960s, then shot up to 66 inches in the early 1970s, where it seems to have stayed. In the same period, busts have been gradually declining, from 36.5 to 34.8, with hips following an almost identical path about three-quarters of an inch behind. Waists gradually increased from 22.2 inches to almost 24, before taking a sudden dive back to 22.5 in the mid-1980s.

Interestingly, a 1983 *Playboy* readers' survey indicated that nearly as many men consider a woman's sexiest feature to be her 'ass' as her breasts, while in the same year 'a *Glamour* magazine non-random sample of 100 men . . . when asked their favourite female body part, chose buttocks over breasts by more than two-to-one.'

Finally, we cannot leave this topic without a small mention of sex within marriage (or at least a stable relationship). All of the preceding has been dealing with attempts at initiating sex on a date with someone whose likely reaction is to a large degree unknown. Do things get better or worse as familiarity begins to play an increasing part?

In Byers and Heinlein (1989), 22 males and 55 females in stable relationships kept detailed records of every instance of sexual initiation, and the response obtained, *also including every time they had considered initiating sex, but had decided not to.*

The results showed that, as in the early stages of a relationship, men both initiate and think about initiating sex more often than women do. An interesting result, however, was that if you take into account the relative number of initiations made by men and women, there were no differences in response pattern.

In other words, men only receive more refusals to their sexual overtures because they make them more often.

Comparing the overall results with subjects' responses on a sexual satisfaction questionnaire, they discovered, not unsurprisingly, that less sexually satisfied subjects were more likely to give a negative response to their partner's initiation of sexual activity. Whether they would be more sexually satisfied if they gave fewer negative responses remains an open question.

Christopher (1988) went into more details about what sexual behaviours women were forced into and how they were forced into them. A sample of 290 single women students filled in an Inventory of Sexual Pressure Dynamics 'developed to assess different aspects of dyadic interactions when sexual pressure occurs'.

He was building on the earlier work of Koss and Oros (1982) who had reported that about a quarter of dating women had their breasts forcibly fondled, and that 20 per cent had engaged in intercourse when the man said things that later proved to be untrue, such as that he loved the woman, or that he was willing to form a relationship only if they were to engage in sex. Christopher gave each woman a list of 21 items and asked whether they had been pressured into them and if so what type of pressure was applied: positive statements, physical attempts, verbal threats or actual force.

In all, 95.3 per cent of the women reported that they had

been pressured into at least one behaviour, with 'Manipulate female breasts over clothes' the favourite at 68.7 per cent (18.5 per cent of whom were talked into it, 77.8 per cent coerced by physical attempts, 2.1 per cent by verbal threats and 1.6 per cent by actual force). The next highest were 'One minute continuous lip kissing' (57.1 per cent mostly by physical attempts), 'Manipulate female genitals over clothes' (56.7 per cent again mostly physical) and 'Oral contact with male genitals' (56.4 per cent almost equally divided into positive statements and physical attempts). Only 6.2 per cent had been pressured into 'Mutual oral manipulation to mutual orgasm'.

The women were also asked the nature of the relationship with the person doing the pressuring: was he a stranger, a friend, were they casually dating, were they seriously dating, or were they engaged? And finally they were asked what was the impact on the relationship: did it improve, get worse or stay the same?

It is a testament to the resilience of relationships that being pressured into mutual oral manipulation to mutual orgasm had the effect of improving 35.5 per cent of relationships in which it happened with only 23.5 per cent getting worse as a result. The only other two forms of pressurized sexual activity which appear, on these figures, to improve relationships are 'Oral contact with female genitals' and 'Sexual intercourse face-to-back'.

The figures suggest that women involved in casual relationships find it easier to resist pressure than those who are seriously dating.

> What may occur in these situations is that the women were willing to give in to sexual pressures while seriously dating because they felt that if they did not, it would result in the man terminating the relationship, an outcome the women may not have wanted. In less serious relationships there was little or no investment to protect.

So men will have a better chance of success trying to fondle

Men will have a better chance of success trying to fondle the breasts of women with whom they are seriously dating

the breasts of women with whom they are seriously dating, than those of casual acquaintances, even though neither group may want it.

'The findings of this study suggest a need to examine our conceptualization of dating and its accompanying sexual interaction.'

We end this chapter with a historical digression relating to something only briefly touched upon and scarcely fondled at all by Byers and Lewis (1988): the location of seduction. The Somerset Quarter Session Rolls provide ample evidence of illicit goings on in the seventeenth century, from which Quaife (1979) was able to determine some very clear patterns.

The initial seduction of a spinster was more likely in summer than in winter (by a ratio of approximately 3 to 2), most frequently in his house, or in the house of one of her relatives.

Within the house, the kitchen and the hall rivalled the bedroom. Floor, bench and table were often more accessible than the bed. The kitchen floor, in front of the fire, was especially popular. Privacy before a winter's fire was scarcely possible but this was not an impediment to sexual activity.

Whereas only a sixth of all seductions took place in outhouses, the stable was especially popular in winter.

Birth statistics also enable conclusions to be drawn about the months in which conception took place and, by inference, the months of greatest sexual activity. The results identify April to August as the period of greatest fecundity, with September to March below average. 'For every two acts of intercourse in October, there were three in June.'

Illegitimacy records provide an almost exact parallel to these figures, with June the most popular and October and November the least popular months for conceiving out of wedlock. The holiday of Jamestide (24 July) was the date on which 11 per cent of maidens lost their virginity.

The interplay between religious holidays and sex is also reflected in the preferred day of the week for seductions: almost 25 per cent of all those between 1640 and 1659 for which a precise date is known occurred on a Sunday, and initial seductions were very unlikely to happen on Tuesday, as the following table verifies:

Somerset Seductions 1640–59 by day of week	Sun	Mon	Tue	Wed	Thur	Fri	Sat
All Seductions	24.7	13.0	10.5	11.7	10.1	14.6	15.4
Initial Seductions	26.4	16.8	4.0	8.0	9.6	15.2	20.0

References and further reading

Burt, M.R. (1980): 'Cultural myths and support for rape'. *J. Pers. Soc. Psychol.* (38) 217–30.

Byers, E.S. (1980): 'Female communication of consent and non-consent to sexual intercourse'. *J. New Brunswick Psychological Assoc.* (5) 12–18.

Byers, E.S. (1988): 'Effects of sexual arousal on men's and women's behavior in sexual disagreement situations'. *J. Sex Research* (25) 235–54.

Byers, E.S. and Heinlein, L. (1989): 'Predicting initiations and refusals of sexual activity in married and cohabiting heterosexual couples'. *J. Sex Research* (26) 210–31.

Byers, E.S. and Lewis, K. (1988): 'Dating couples' disagreements over the desired level of sexual intimacy'. *J. Sex Research* (24) 15–29.

Byers, E.S. and Wilson, P. (1985): 'Accuracy of women's expectations regarding men's responses to refusals of sexual advances in dating situations'. *Int. J. Women's Studies* (4) 376–87.

Christopher, F.S. (1988): 'An initial investigation into a continuum of premarital sexual pressure'. *J. Sex Research* (25) 255–66.

Corcoran, K.J. and Thomas, L.R. (1991): 'The influence of observed alcohol consumption on perceptions of initiation of sexual activity in a college dating situation'. *J. App. Social Psychology* (21) 500–7.

Ehrmann, W.W. (1959): *Premarital Dating Behavior*. Holt, NY.

Jesser, C.J. (1978): 'Male responses to direct verbal sexual initiatives of females'. *J. Sex Research* (14) 118–28.

Kaats, G.R. and Davis, K.E. (1970): 'The dynamics of sexual behavior of college students'. *J. Marriage Family* (32) 390–99.

Koss, M.P. and Oros, C.J. (1982): 'Sexual experiences survey: A research instrument investigating sexual aggression and victimization'. *J. Consulting and Clinical Psychology* (55) 162–70.

Lewis, R.A. and Burr, W.R. (1975) 'Premarital coitus and commitment among college students'. *Archives of Sexual Behav.* (4) 73–9.

McCormick, N.B. (1979): 'Come-ons and put-offs: Unmarried students' strategies for having and avoiding sexual intercourse'. *Psychology of Women Quarterly* (4) 195–211.

Mazur, A. (1986): 'US trends in feminine beauty and over-adaptation'. *J. Sex Research* (22) 281–303.

Peplau, L.A., Rubin, Z. and Hill, C.T. (1977): 'Sexual intimacy in dating relationships'. *J. Social Issues* (33) 86–109.

Perper, T. and Weis, D.L. (1987): 'Proceptive and rejective strategies of US and Canadian college women'. *J. Sex Research* (23) 455–80.

Quaife, G.R. (1979): *Wanton Wenches and Wayward Wives (Peasants and Illicit Sex in Early Seventeenth-Century England).* Croom Helm.

Smith, J.E., Waldorf, V.A. and Trembath, D.L. (1990): 'Single white male looking for thin, very attractive . . .'. *Sex Roles* (23) 11–12.

Strouse, J.S. (1987): 'College bars as social settings for heterosexual contacts'. *J. Sex Research* (23) 344–82.

7

Sex By Numbers

In common with many other fields in the behavioural sciences, sex research sets itself a fundamental objective of finding more about who does what to whom and why, and what the likely effects will be. In all such areas, the questionnaire (often loosely and inaccurately referred to as 'personality test') has proved to be indispensable.

The list that follows is by no means exhaustive, but gives a flavour of the volume of work that has been undertaken in order to provide reliable measures of various aspects of people's sexual inclinations:

Bem Sex-Role Inventory
Derogatis Sexual Functioning Inventory
Effeminacy Scale
Eysenck Inventory of Attitudes to Sex
Feminine Gender Identity Scale
Golombok–Rust Inventory of Sexual Satisfaction
Herpes Attitudes Scale
Herpes Knowledge Scale
Heterosexual Behavior Inventory
Heterosexual Interest and Experience Scale
Heterosexual–Homosexual Rating Scale
Imaginal Processes Inventory
Index of Marital Satisfaction
Index of Sexual Satisfaction
Marital Adjustment Scale

Negative Attitudes Towards Masturbation Inventory
O'Brien Multiphasic Narcissism Inventory
Pinney Sexual Satisfaction Inventory
Premarital Sexual Permissiveness Scale
Rape Myth Acceptance Scale
Rate of Homosexual Development Scale
Sensation Seeking Scale
Sex-Guilt Subscale
Sex Inventory
Sexual Activity and Preference Scale
Sexual Arousability Inventory
Sexual Arousability Index
Sexual Attitude Scale
Sexual Compatibility Test
Sexual Interaction Inventory
Sexual Interest Questionnaire
Sexual Knowledge and Attitude Test
Sexual Opinion Survey
Sexual Orientation Method
Sexual Responsiveness Survey
Sex-Role Ideology Scale
Sexuality Scale
Wilson Sexual Fantasy Questionnaire

There are many reasons for the existence of so many measures. For one thing, they may be designed for different purposes. The Herpes Attitude Inventory, to take one specific example, was designed in 1985 to provide a measure of the moral viewpoint a respondent took regarding genital herpes.

It comprised forty statements, with each of which the respondent was invited to indicate his or her level of agreement on a five-point scale ranging from Strongly Agree to Strongly Disagree. Typical items were:

1 The thought of genital herpes is disgusting.
7 If I had a roommate with genital herpes, I would move out.

16 A person who has genital herpes got what s/he deserves.
20 I would consider marrying someone who has genital herpes.
31 People who have genital herpes should never have sex again.
38 I could discuss genital herpes with my parents.

The least useful items on the scale turned out to be 'I would feel self-conscious if I got genital herpes' (with which most respondents agreed) and 'You can tell that someone has genital herpes just by looking at them' (with which most disagreed).

In parallel with the Herpes Attitude Inventory was developed the Herpes Knowledge Scale, a test of factual knowledge about the disease. This measure comprised 54 items about herpes, some correct, some incorrect. The respondent had to reply with 'true', 'false' or 'don't know' to items such as:

'I would feel self-conscious if I got genital herpes'

19 People who wear contact lenses and have oral (mouth) herpes should avoid putting the lenses in their mouths because the herpes infection could spread to their eyes.
28 Genital herpes can be contagious even if the herpes sore has a scab on it.
50 The best way to treat genital herpes sores is to keep them moist.

One of the reasons for developing separate scales of knowledge and attitudes towards herpes was to see to what extent people's accurate knowledge of the disease affected attitudes towards it. The results of an early study (Bruce and McLaughlin, 1986) produced only a very low correlation between knowledge and attitude, though some patterns began to emerge about knowledge in certain areas possibly affecting personal attitude towards coping with the disease.

There was clearly a need for further validations studies and 'further research must also be aimed at analyzing the underlying factor structure of both scales'.

But just as this was ready to roll, AIDS came along and everyone seemed to lose interest in herpes completely.

Few measures are as specialized as the Herpes Attitudes Inventory and Herpes Knowledge Scale. What most researchers are looking for in a questionnaire is something that will give a reliable picture of a respondent's sexual orientation, attitudes and experience. There are still a large number of different tests that aim to cover those aspects, which seems to suggest a strong preference among researchers for developing their own measures rather than picking up other people's used devices and re-using them.

Nurius and Hudson (1988) decided to tackle the problem of sex-questionnaire proliferation by producing the Sexual Activity and Preference Scale, 'a new multidimensional measure of sexual activity and preference'. Their new measure contained six subscales relating to amounts of sexual activity and six subscales related to degrees of preference.

They started, as did so many before them, by making out a list of things people can do to each other in a sexual context. 'In developing the measure, it became necessary to create items that were behaviorally very explicit. The aim was to eliminate or to minimize ambiguity concerning the type of sexual activity being identified.'

The final list of items was meant to provide a complete taxonomy of sexual activity. Despite their desire for completeness, however, they did feel constrained not to stray too far into certain areas:

Several types of sexual activity were initially tested and discarded because of their infrequency of occurrence or because their inclusion was so offensive to respondents that many refused to participate in the research or would not provide accurate and candid responses. These included incest, rape, bestiality and necrophilia.

Their *a priori* analysis of sexual practice led to the categorization of all sexual activities under the following headings:

1 Heterosexual activity (with partner of opposite sex)
2 Homosexual activity (with partner of same sex)
3 Autosexual activity (without partner)
4 Multiple partners (not necessarily at the same time)
5 Anal activity
6 Oral activity (involving oral-genital stimulation)
7 Donor activity (providing sexual gratification to partner)
8 Recipient activity (receiving gratification from partner)
9 Cross-masturbation (mutual sexual fondling)
10 Genital activity (mutual genital contact)
11 Locational variety (sex in a variety of places)
12 Feminist variety (women adopting a more active role)

They then drew up their list of 78 items, classifying each one to its corresponding scale or scales in the above categories. Each respondent was asked to fill in replies in two columns, indicating in the first column how frequently he or she indulged in that particular behaviour, and in the second column how frequently he or she would like to indulge in it.

In both cases, a five-point scale was to be used:

1=never 2=rarely 3=occasionally 4=fairly often 5=very often.

Here is a randomly selected sample of the items:

Women adopting a more active role

1 I feel or stroke my own genitals until I become very sexually excited.
4 I have sex with strangers.
7 A woman kisses, licks or sucks my anus.
13 A man inserts his penis in my anus and moves it in and out until he comes.
22 I have sex on a boat.
30 I have sex with a close friend.
32 I kiss, lick or suck a woman's clitoris or vagina until she becomes very sexually excited.
45 I have sex while swimming.

57 (for men only) I slide my penis in and out of a woman's vagina until I become very sexually excited.
60 (women only) A man rubs his penis around the lips of my vagina until I come.
75 (women only) I become sexually aroused when I undress a man.

After 689 volunteers, mostly from Hawaii, had completed the questionnaire anonymously ('participants were instructed to look through the questionnaire before deciding to participate'), the analytic task began to determine patterns of responding and to see whether these patterns confirmed the existence of twelve sexual dimensions as hypothesized above.

The result could well be summarized as a draw: six of the dimensions were confirmed as independent factors, with the other six found to be no more than varieties of homosexual and heterosexual activity. So you should now go back to the earlier list and cross out Oral, Donor, Recipient, Cross-masturbation, Genital and Feminist

'I have sex on a boat'

activities as having no statistically independent worth of their own.

Everything within the scope of the study (the authors again take pains to point out that masochism, incest, bestiality, sadism, transvestism and certain other behaviours are excluded from consideration) is already covered in the six categories: Sex with men, Sex with women, Autosexual, Multiple partners (including sex with a stranger), Anal and Locational.

> For the male sample, the first factor, which measures sexual activity with a male partner, emerged as a measure of homosexual activity, and the second factor, which measures sexual activity with a female partner, emerged as a measure of heterosexual activity. For the female sample, this pattern was reversed.

That is reassuring.

Whether homosexuality and heterosexuality are opposite ends of the same scale, as some maintain, or are truly independent preference states (as bisexuals would prefer to think of them) is still an open question, though the authors incline to the second view. Since the new questionnaire provides scores for Homosexual (HOM) and Heterosexual (HET) Activity (A) and Preference (P), the researchers point out that it is possible to compute a Relative Activity Orientation (RAO) to provide a measure between 0 and 1 of precisely how Homosexual you are, according to the following formula, which expresses the amount of homosexual activity as a fraction of total sexual activity:

$$RAO = HOMA/(HOMA + HETA)$$

and similarly, a Relative Preference Orientation (RPO) is given by:

$$RPO = HOMP/(HOMP + HETP)$$

What the authors do not discuss in any great detail is differences in activity scores (how much an item is practised) and preference scores (how much the respondent would like to do it). This would appear to be a fruitful field for further research.

Further possible levels of refinement have been provided by Mosher, Barton-Henry and Green (1988) who developed a new method for investigating subjective sexual arousal. Their subjects were invited to relax and then indulge in four separate fantasies in turn:

Heterosexual Recall – Remembering the last time they had engaged in heterosexual petting or intercourse, including all relevant details, experiences and emotions;

Masturbation Recall – As above but with an episode of masturbation;

Free Fantasy – Imagining any sexual fantasy they want to;

Guided Fantasy – Selecting your ideal sex partner and imagining a sexual encounter, including petting and coitus.

After each fantasy, they were asked to assess how they felt during the experience on eleven separate factors, each to be rated on a 7-point scale. The factors were Sexual Arousal, Genital Sensations, Sexual Warmth, Muscular Tension, Non-genital Physical Sensations, Sexual Absorption, Sexual Tension, Sex Drive, Sexual Deprivation, Sexual Goal Value and Sexual Interest.

Next, another questionnaire was produced on which the subjects recorded an amplification of their response to the second item on this list, Genital Sensations. The instructions began: 'Genital sensations refer to sensory sensations in the genital region that accompany and are a source of somatogenic or psychogenic sexual stimulation and that are a function of increasing vasocongestion in the genital area', then went on to talk about erections and engorgement of the labia, before finally asking the subject to indicate the peak level of genital sensation they felt during the fantasy experience.

This level had to be marked on a scale comprising the following 11 points:

1 No genital sensations.
2 Onset of genital sensations – onset of swelling of penis or of vulva or nipple erection.
3 Mild genital sensations – vasocongestion sufficient to begin penile erection or to begin vaginal lubrication.
4 Moderate genital sensations – vasocongestion sufficient to erect penis fully or to lubricate vagina fully.
5 Prolonged moderate genital sensations – maintaining erection or lubrication for several minutes.
6 Intense genital sensations – hard or pulsing erection and elevation of testicles in the scrotum; or receptive, engorged vagina or sex flush, or breast swelling or retraction of clitoris or ballooning of vagina.
7 Prolonged intense genital sensations – near orgasmic levels of genital sensations; swelling of head of penis or high levels of muscular tension or heavy breathing or high heart rate; lasting several minutes and will produce orgasm if continued.
8 Mild orgasm – 3–5 contractions
9 Moderate orgasm – 5–8 contractions
10 Intense orgasm – 8–12 contractions
11 Multiple orgasm

And lastly, the subjects were asked to complete a checklist of 50 adjectives, saying whether each was appropriate to describe their state. Among the 50 adjectives, the important ones (embedded randomly among 40 camouflage items) were: lustful, sexually erotic, sexually aroused, sensuous, turned-on, sexually hot, horny, sexy, passionate and sexually excited.

Strong correlations between responses in these various scales all confirm their validity as measures of various aspects of sexual arousal.

Imagining any sexual fantasy they want to

But is it really worth going to all this trouble? After all, six scales on a sex test of three separate measures just of subjective arousal, might seem rather over-indulgent. In real life, you might ask, does it not all boil down to a simple question of whether someone likes sex or not?

What you would be talking about then is the *affect-evaluation* portion of the theoretical model of sexual behaviour. Whatever aspect of our behaviour we are discussing, we must consider our *affective* (conditioned responses to stimuli or cues), *informational* (based on knowledge and beliefs) and *imaginal* (based on fantasy or imagination) dispositions and these may all interfere with each other. Our affective responses turn into evaluative and attitudinal strategies, which may then be modified by information or imagination.

So the affect-evaluative is the most basic level of disposition and, in the field of sexual behaviour, it has been equated with the construct dimension called Erotophobia-Erotophilia. Fisher, Byrne, White and Kelley (1988) investigated Erotophobia-Erotophilia as a dimension of personality.

'The first step in the measurement process was the generation of 53 items that were intended to assess affective-evaluative responses to a range of sexual themes.' The next step was to get 88 male and 103 female students to respond to the 53 items, then to look at 19 erotic slides and to rate their reactions.

By correlating the responses to the questionnaire with the responses to the erotic slides, the experimenters were able to see how well the questionnaire items could predict whether people would enjoy looking at dirty pictures.

Once again, they produced an original set of 53 items. Here are a few we have not met before:

1 I think it would be very entertaining to look at hard-core pornography.
6 If people thought I was interested in oral sex, I would be embarrassed.
14 Watching a gogo dancer of the opposite sex would not be very exciting.
16 When I think of seeing pictures of someone of the same sex as myself masturbating, it nauseates me.
18 Manipulating my genitals would not be an arousing experience.

As usual, all items had to be marked on a 7-point scale, ranging from 'I strongly agree' to 'I strongly disagree'.

Later, the gogo dancer in item 14 was replaced by a stripper.

Correlations were good between scores on the Erotophobia-Erotophilia measure and reactions to dirty pictures, and further correlations with other measures of personality revealed more aspects of erotophiliacs (those who like sex) and erotophobes (those with a comparative dislike or fear of sex).

'In several respects, erotophobic males possess socially valuable characteristics (achievement, order, endurance) that connote adherence to the "work ethic" while erotophiliac men tend to be located at the opposite end of this dimension.'

Erotophiliac women were also low on achievement aspirations, but showed up high on measures of personal understanding. They are also more likely to breast-feed their infants.

Both male and female erotophiliacs masturbate more frequently than erotophobes. They also have greater sexual experience and more partners and erotophiliac males are more likely to be present at the birth of their children.

Perhaps with all this having sex, masturbating, attending wives in labour or breast-feeding, erotophiliacs simply do not have time for achievement aspiration and work ethic too.

We cannot leave this subject without mentioning correlations between sex-questionnaires of the type discussed above and standard personality measures. Husted and Edwards (1976) explored the relationship between the sexual behaviour of 20 male subjects and their scores on the Minnesota Multiphasic Personality Inventory (MMPI) and the Sensation Seeking Scale (SSS). Specifically, they were interested in total number of sexual partners, number of ejaculations over a given period, number of spontaneous erections, masturbatory erections, masturbatory ejaculations, erections with partner and ejaculations without partner, all of which were correlated with the personality measures.

> For older subjects, more experienced in sexual relationships, the only subscale of the SSS that correlated with number of sexual partners was the Boredom Susceptibility scale. This scale measures 'dislike of repetition' and a 'restless reaction to monotony' and apparently is reflected in a need for a variety of sexual partners.

Introverts tend to masturbate more than extroverts 'but there is not a concomitant reduction in heterosexual activity'.

Depression has a positive relationship with both sexual arousal and masturbatory behaviour 'indicating that masturbation may be an important means of tension reduction for the depressed'.

We must finally mention the results of Anderson, Broffitt, Karlsson and Turnquist (1989) who analysed the results of the Sexual Arousability Index after it had been administered four times to each of 57 sexually active women and 66 women undergoing gynaecological surgery. The internal results of the study were good: the re-test reliability was very high, indicating that people's scores on the test are quite stable, and a content analysis of the responses confirmed six different domains of sexual arousability. These were Seduction, Body Caressing, Oral-genital and Genital Stimulation, Intercourse, Masturbation and Erotic media. The only problem with the questionnaire was that:

'The SAI, like other psychological measures, was poor in predicting a criterion (the occurrence of inhibited sexual excitement).'

So the Sexual Arousability Index would seem to work very well, except if you want it to provide a guide to sexual arousability.

References and further reading

Anderson, B.L., Broffitt, B., Karlsson, J.A. and Turnquist, D.C. (1989): 'A psychometric analysis of the Sexual Arousability Index'. *J. Consult. Clin. Psychology* (57) 123–30.

Bruce, K.E.M. and McLaughlin, J. (1986): 'The development of scales to assess knowledge and attitudes about genital herpes'. *J. Sex Research* (22) 73–84.

Fisher, W.A., Byrne, D., White, L.A. and Kelley, K. (1988): 'Erotophobia-Erotophilia as a dimension of personality'. *J. Sex Research* (25) 123–51.

Husted, J.R. and Edwards, A.E. (1976): 'Personality correlates of male sexual arousal and behavior'. *Archives of Sexual Behav.* (5) 149–56.

LoPiccolo, J. and Steger, J.C. (1974): 'The sexual interaction inventory: A new instrument for assessment of sexual dysfunction'. *Archives of Sexual Behav.* (3) 585–95.

Mosher, D.L., Barton-Henry, M. and Green, S.E. (1988): 'Subjective sexual arousal and involvement: Development of multiple indicators'. *J. Sex Research* (24) 412–25.

Nurius, P.R. and Hudson, W.W. (1988): 'Sexual activity and preference: Six quantifiable dimensions'. *J. Sex Research* (24) 1988.

Thorne, F.C. (1973): 'The sex inventory'. *J. Consult. Clin. Psychology* (22) 367–87.

Zuckerman, M. (1973): 'Scales for sex experience for males and females'. *J. Consult. Clin. Psychology* (41) 28–9.

8

Onan the Barbarian

And it came to pass at that time, that Judah went down from his brethren, and turned in to a certain Adullamite, whose name was Hirah. And Judah saw there a daughter of a certain Canaanite, whose name was Shuah; and he took her, and went in unto her.

And she conceived, and bare a son; and he called his name Er. And she conceived again and bare a son; and she called his name Onan. And she yet again conceived, and bare a son; and she called his name Shelah; and he was at Chezib, when she bare him.

And Judah took a wife for Er his firstborn, whose name was Tamar. And Er, Judah's firstborn, was wicked in the sight of the LORD; and the LORD slew him.

And Judah said unto Onan, 'Go in unto thy brother's wife and marry her, and raise up seed to thy brother.' And Onan knew that the seed should not be his; and it came to pass, when he went in unto his brother's wife, that he spilled it on the ground, lest that he should give seed to his brother. And the thing which he did displeased the LORD: whereupon he slew him also.

Genesis, Ch. 38.

Ever since the Lord slew Onan for spilling his seed, masturbation has had a bad reputation. Indeed, even in today's enlightened times, there still seems a reluctance to talk about it. Onan himself does not merit an entry in

Chambers Biographical Dictionary, or in the Biblical Glossary of *Pears Cyclopaedia*, and both the Cambridge and Macmillan encyclopedias, move hurriedly on from Onager to Onassis. So no excuses are offered for Onan's sin (though one might perhaps expect rather odd behaviour from a man with two brothers called Er and Shelah).

Indeed, perhaps the only homage in living memory to the eponym of Onanism came from the American humorist Dorothy Parker, who called her parrot Onan because it too spilt its seed on the ground.

With this sort of historical background, it is no surprise that the world's most frequently indulged in sexual activity should also be one of the least openly discussed. And this has, of course, made it an additional challenge for any intrepid researcher who has dared to enter this highly charged area.

And it came to pass that Abramson and Mosher (1975) did put together a questionnaire. And they saw that it was good, so they called its name NATMI, which is to say the Negative Attitudes Towards Masturbation Inventory.

NATMI was designed to measure feelings of guilt induced by masturbation and belief in negative myths associated with masturbation. What they found was that negative attitudes towards masturbation were associated with lower frequencies of masturbation.

As LoPresto, Sherman and Sherman (1985) point out, 'This interplay among attitudes, guilt and behavior appears to support Izard's conceptualization of sex guilt as an affective-cognitive structure consisting of sexual cognitions and affective and behavioral dispositions that inhibit sexual behavior judged immoral by the individual.'

In other words, if it makes you feel guilty, you don't do it.

With other writers, such as Greenberg and Archambault (1973) showing a connection between masturbatory guilt and low self-esteem, and various studies demonstrating that most adolescent males are indoctrinated with societal and religious exaggerations and myths concerning masturbation, it is perhaps surprising that anyone does it at all. Though it should be mentioned here that, according to DeMartino (1974), 'in women with high IQs, significant correlations were found between an acceptance of masturbation and both high feelings of self-esteem and high feelings of security.'

Miller and Lief (1976) used a questionnaire to determine the masturbatory beliefs and habits of high school, college and medical student samples totalling 556 students. Their results showed that:

- Males in high school and college have more liberal attitudes towards masturbation than do females, but female graduate students are more liberal than males.
- Those who have never masturbated are more conservative than those who have.
- About 16 per cent of medical students believe that masturbation is a cause of emotional and mental illness.
- 97 per cent of males and 78 per cent of females masturbate.
- 19 per cent of females masturbated before age ten, 34 per cent before thirteen, and 45 per cent before sixteen.
- 76 per cent of all subjects felt that masturbation is healthy.

Whatever medical students may think (and apparently hospital residents are even stronger in the belief that masturbation is bad for you), almost all sexologists take a positive view of masturbation. DeMartino (1979) even goes so far as to maintain that 'its lack of use may be associated with the presence of emotional problems'.

Yet adolescents themselves are still confused, which was what led LoPresto, Sherman and Sherman to investigate the potential benefits of masturbation seminars:

> The present study was designed to determine whether course instruction for adolescent males which dealt specifically with masturbation a) increased positive attitudes towards masturbation in general, b) diminished false beliefs about the harmful nature of masturbation (sex myths), and/or c) reduced affectively experienced sex guilt

. . . it was also reasoned that a change in attitudes towards masturbation would in turn effect a change in behavior (masturbation frequency).

So 198 male (they limited the instruction to an all-male group in order to reduce possible embarrassment) students (mainly fifteen-year-olds) at a Catholic high school in Maryland, were taught about masturbation after having their attitudes assessed on the NATMI.

Apart from the 30 items on NATMI, the researchers report that an additional 110 items covering a wide range of sexually related topics were also included. The question 'When I masturbate, it is generally about — times per week' was added as a self-report of masturbation frequency.

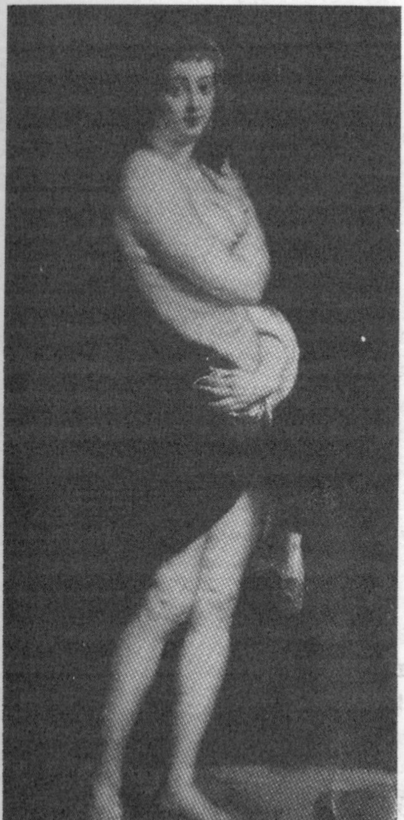

'I feel guilty about masturbation'

The 30 NATMI questions cover three aspects of attitudes towards masturbation. Factor 1 (positive attitudes) is represented by such items as 'Masturbation can provide an outlet for sexual fantasies without harming anyone else or endangering oneself' or 'Masturbation can provide harmless relief from sexual tension'. Factor 2 (false beliefs) has statements such as 'Masturbation can lead to homosexuality' or 'People who masturbate will not enjoy sexual intercourse as much as those who refrain from masturbation'; and Factor 3 (personally experienced negative effects) is things like 'When I masturbate, I am disgusted with myself' or simply 'I feel guilty about masturbation'.

The 40-minute seminar on masturbation, which formed the main part of this experiment, was included at the end of the first week of a month-long sex education programme. The experimental group went to the lecture, while a control group discussed homosexuality instead.

The masturbation seminar was informal, and covered the following themes:

1 That masturbation is extremely common among adolescents.
2 That many commonly held negative views about masturbation are incorrect.
3 That masturbation can be a perfectly acceptable alternative to sexual intercourse, without the risk of pregnancy or venereal disease.
4 That masturbation is a good way to learn about one's sexual responses and rehearsing for the real thing.
5 That certain societal and religious influences may make people feel guilty about masturbation.

After another two weeks, all experimental subjects were asked to fill in the expanded NATMI questionnaire again, on the pretext that earlier results had been inadvertently discarded.

The results were interesting, and not totally in line with expectations. According to their scores on NATMI, a 40-minute lecture on the joys and benefits of masturbation did have an influence on students' attitudes towards it. After the lecture, they had greater positive attitudes towards masturbation and fewer false beliefs about the harmful effects of masturbation. But they still felt just as guilty about it as they had before.

When pre-seminar and post-seminar masturbation frequencies were compared, they discovered a *decrease* from

4.94 to 4.84 times a week. They then massaged the figures a little:

> However, when the scores of individuals who reported a frequency of masturbation greater than 15 times per week were eliminated (because we felt that some of these outliers were quite unreasonable, e.g., 40 times per week), the pretest mean became 3.65 . . . and the post-test mean became 3.64.

One must, however, doubt the methodological justifiability of eliminating supposed exaggerators while not attempting to take account of under-estimators. Indeed, with 15 per cent claiming not to masturbate at all, it could be argued that there are grounds for eliminating some figures at the other end of the scale.

The fact that the seminar appeared to alter some aspects of an individual's masturbatory beliefs, but not others, brought forth some interesting explanations:

> Since post-testing in the present study was completed only two weeks following treatment, changes in subjects' affective responses may have been prematurely assessed. It is also possible, however, given the Catholic Church's strong position on masturbation, that these predominantly Catholic adolescents would experience more guilt (in spite of changed general attitudes and fewer false beliefs) than other subjects might.

On the other hand, an in many ways opposite argument is offered for the ineffectiveness of the seminar to change masturbation levels:

> There is a possibility that increases in masturbatory frequency were not reported because subjects were already masturbating at fairly high levels . . . The current data may reflect a maximum level of arousal which would preclude significant increases despite a reduction in

negative attitudes. Furthermore, these adolescents may simply not have had the opportunity to engage in masturbation more often, due to daily schedules and living arrangements.

There is also some doubt expressed about the wording of the question on masturbation frequency, which may not have been clear enough to obtain valid post-experiment estimates of changed behaviour.

In other words, they were masturbating so much that they couldn't possibly want to do it any more, and anyway they didn't have time to do it any more even if they wanted to, and a lot of them were probably lying about their masturbation frequencies, and they probably didn't understand the question.

These excuses look a little flimsy.

The researchers close their paper with the usual insistence that more research is necessary: '*The further investigation of masturbation and its ramifications for the adolescent seems well-warranted in light of the present findings.*'

We move on to female masturbation.

'To determine the relationship between masturbatory and coital behavior, 117 middle-class female volunteers were classified into three styles of masturbatory behavior – direct, indirect and non-masturbators.'

So began Leff and Israel (1983) in their important work on the effects of different techniques of female masturbation. Direct masturbation, they explain, is defined as the direct digital manipulation of the clitoris or use of a vibrator. Indirect masturbation includes all other methods of masturbation not defined as direct.

The need for some form of national instruction in masturbation became clear early in the survey, when they discovered that 70 per cent of masturbators reported no change in their masturbatory style from that of their initial masturbatory experiences.

This may not matter, however, since no relationship was

found between coital orgasmic capacity and masturbatory style.

What they did find was that non-masturbators achieved orgasm in coitus via additional clitoral stimulation significantly less frequently than either direct or indirect masturbators.

It would seem from this fact that a gentleman engaged in coitus with a lady should first ascertain whether she is a masturbator or non-masturbator before taking the decision whether or not to provide additional clitoral stimulation.

Not surprisingly, it was found that 'direct masturbators have a significantly greater preference for clitoral, as opposed to vaginal, stimulation as a means of achieving orgasm.'

So perhaps our perfect gentleman should also ask whether his paramour is a direct or indirect masturbator.

Whatever the answer, however, he should not take it as immutable, for attitudes towards masturbation are subject to change and education, as a study published in the journal *Adolescence* (vol. 23 pp.773–92) in 1988 showed. Entitled 'Changing auto-erotic attitudes and practices among college females: A two-year follow-up study', it reported the results of questionnaires given to 22 female and 9 male undergraduates enrolled on a 'functional marriage and family' course in Wisconsin, and 18 female and 2 male undergraduates on other courses.

Comparing results of the sexual attitudes questionnaire given at the start of the course and two years later, they found that 'college experience had a liberating effect on women in general', but the subjects who attended sex education classes in the marriage and family course were 'substantially more accepting of masturbation by both male and female acquaintances' and were more likely to believe it to be healthy. Also, the percentage of women in this group who had ever engaged in masturbation was significantly higher after two years than it had been at the start of the course.

Indirect masturbation includes all other methods not defined as direct

Griffitt (1975) discovered an interesting fact about masturbation, and its different role for men and women, in the course of a more wide-ranging experiment. He had 30 male and 30 female subjects (ages 18–23) watch six photographic slides which depicted, respectively, ventral-ventral intercourse, fellatio, cunnilingus, dorsal-ventral intercourse, partially nude heterosexual petting, and masturbation (with the masturbator the same sex as the subject).

They were asked how arousing they found each slide, and how much they had personally indulged in the activity portrayed. One of the intentions of the research was to discover the relationship between sexual experience and arousability.

The surprising finding was that among males, masturbation experience was the only factor of sexual behaviour that was a general predictor of arousability: the more you masturbate, the more you are aroused by dirty pictures.

With the female subjects, however, every individual item of sexual experience acted as a pointer towards arousability.

Their amount of fellatio experience was the best guide to general arousability, followed by ventral-ventral intercourse and cunnilingus. Masturbatory experience was worst of all.

It was, however, true for both sexes that 'sexual experience and responsiveness are activity-specific', i.e., the more you have performed a particular activity, the more arousing you are likely to find it. It was particularly true that the men who had greatest experience of heterosexual fellatio were the ones who enjoyed the fellatio slide most.

Taken altogether, these findings would seem to suggest that men masturbate because they like sex, but women masturbate because they like masturbating.

Finally, having disposed of boys masturbating and women masturbating, we conclude with a discussion of two pieces of research in which both sexes did it. In Fisher, Pollack and Malatesta (1986) masturbation played a key role in a series of experiments designed to detect differences in male and female patterns of sexual arousal.

'Twenty-four men and 18 women participated in experimental sessions during which they masturbated to orgasm while viewing sexually explicit films and then rated the film for its arousal value.'

The main variables of the experiment were therefore the time it took the subjects to reach orgasm (the orgasm latency) and the subjectively assessed arousal value of the film they were watching while doing so.

> Male orgasmic latency was not significantly different across rating categories, whereas female research participants showed a distinct quadratic trend in which films perceived as being *average* in arousal quality resulted in the longest latencies.

So masturbating men reach orgasm in much the same time whatever the quality of the pornography they are watching, but women are quickest when watching either highly arousing or relatively unarousing movies. It is possible, of course, that average porn merely distracts from the job in hand*, slowing down the progress to orgasm, and that poor porn is neither helpful nor distracting, but it is clear that further research is needed. Perhaps the quality of the orgasm should also be considered a dependent variable.

Our second study that involved both male and female masturbation is Hessellund (1976) in which the solitary masturbatory habits of married couples was discussed.

> While there was a significant difference in intercourse frequency among married and unmarried subjects, there were no significant differences in frequency of masturbation between married and unmarried subjects. If masturbation is considered a substitute for intercourse, one would expect that frequency of masturbation would be greater among unmarried subjects than among subjects with daily sexual access to a partner. This hypothesis was not borne out.

That surprising finding came from a survey of 38 contentedly married couples in Denmark. Of these, '15 men and 24 women never masturbate. Among 12 couples both partners independently stated that they never masturbate. Twelve women have husbands who masturbated from seldom [once or twice a year] to daily. Where both spouses masturbate, the husband masturbates more frequently than his wife.'

Generally, their spouses did not know about this behaviour. Of the 11 couples where both partners masturbated, only three pairs shared the knowledge, though five masturbating husbands felt certain that their wives knew.

> When it is possible to hide masturbation from a person as close as a husband or wife this is connected with time and place for masturbatory behaviour . . . More than half

*or vibrator, as the case may be.

of the husbands and more than three-quarters of the wives masturbate in bed when the spouse has fallen asleep.

But men are far more likely to masturbate in the bathroom 'as a matter of routine before brushing their teeth and washing their hands.' The reason for this, the researcher suggests might be 'to dispose of the ejaculate expediently – partly for hygienic/aesthetic reasons and partly for preventing disclosing stains on bedclothes.'

Interestingly, whereas there is a slight negative correlation among men between intercourse frequency and masturbation frequency, the reverse is true of women, i.e. men who have intercourse frequently are likely to masturbate less than men who have intercourse more rarely, but the most prolific female masturbators are also the women who have intercourse most frequently.

Despite this result, Hessellund comes to the tentative conclusion that *'For men masturbation functions more as a supplement to the sexual life, while for women it is to a greater extent a substitute for intercourse.'*

Sadly, even if, as a result of all this research, masturbation is eventually compulsorily taught at all good schools, and accepted as a suitable subject for conversation at the most refined dinner parties, it will all come too late for the complete rehabilitation of poor Onan. For Onan's sin was not, as has become enshrined in language, that of Onanism, but the distinctly less self-indulgent behaviour of coitus interruptus.

References and further reading

Abramson, P.R. (1973): 'The relationship of frequency of masturbation to several aspects of behavior'. *J. Sex Research* (9) 132–42.

Abramson, P.R. and Mosher, D.L. (1975): 'Development of a measure of negative attitudes towards masturbation'. *J. Consult. Clin. Psychology* (43) 485–90.

Arafat, I.S. and Cotton, W.L. (1974): 'Masturbation practices of males and females'. *J. Sex Research* (10) 293–307.

DeMartino, M.F. (1974): *Sex and the Intelligent Woman.* Springer, NY.

DeMartino, M.F. (Ed) (1979): *Human Autoerotic Practices.* Human Sciences Press, NY.

Fisher, T.D., Pollack, R.H. and Malatesta, V.J. (1986): 'Orgasmic latency and subjective ratings of erotic stimuli in male and female subjects'. *J. Sex Research* (22) 85–93.

Greenberg, J.S. and Archambault, F.X. (1973): 'Masturbation and self-esteem'. *J. Sex Research* (9) 41–51.

Griffitt, W. (1975): 'Sexual experience and sexual responsiveness: Sex differences'. *Archives of Sexual Behav.* (4) 529–40.

Hessellund, H. (1976): 'Masturbation and sexual fantasies in married couples'. *Archives of Sexual Behav.* (5) 133–47.

Leff, A.J. and Israel, M. (1983): 'The relationship between mode of female masturbation and achievement of orgasm in coitus'. *Archives of Sexual Behav.* (12) 227–37.

LoPresto, C.T., Sherman, M.F. and Sherman, N. (1985): 'The effects of a masturbation seminar on high school males' attitudes, false beliefs, guilt and behavior'. *J. Sex Research* (21) 142–56.

Miller, W.R. and Lief, H.I. (1976): 'Masturbatory attitudes, knowledge, and experience: Data from the Sex Knowledge and Attitude Test (SKAT)'. *Archives of Sexual Behav.* (5) 447–67.

9

The Oral Tradition

Before proceeding to a discussion of the important findings of Newcomer and Udry (1985) on the incidence of oral sex among adolescents, it is desirable to survey the background to the subject in order to place modern research in a proper historical perspective.

In pre-Christian times, hardly a word was spoken against oral sex. Ever since the prostitutes of ancient Phoenicia first put on lipstick as a means of advertising their expertise at fellatio, such skills have been generally valued. Even Cleopatra and the Emperor Tiberius were praised by ancient Roman writers for their experience and talents at oral sex.

In the fourth century AD, however, things started to go wrong when Christianity spread through the Roman Empire and the Arian heresy lost out to the official church line.

Roughly speaking, the Arian view was that the body is bad and the soul is good, so any non-procreative sexual activity must be good because it releases good spirit without running the risk of creating another body. St Augustine, however, having grown too old to have a personal interest in the matter, laid down the official doctrine that only procreative sex is good.

In the eighteenth century, the official view of the church was described by St Alphonsus Ligori, a Neapolitan lawyer turned saint. In a sex manual written for confessors, in order that they might be prepared for sexual problems that they could encounter in the confessional, he answers the question: 'Is it always a mortal sin, if a husband introduces his penis into the mouth of his wife?'

His answer depends heavily on the idea of 'pollution' (=emission of semen):

> . . . owing to the heat of the mouth there is approximate danger of pollution, and because this appears of itself a new species of luxury, repugnant to nature . . . for as often as another vessel than the natural vessel ordained for copulation, is sought by the man, it seems a new species of luxury.

Finally he comes down in favour of fellatio as long as 'the husband does this to excite himself for natural copulation'.

Despite this limited acceptance of the act by the church, it was still frowned upon in no uncertain terms by the psychoanalyst Richard von Krafft-Ebing in his *Psychopathia Sexualis*:

> Cunnilingus and fellare (the penis in the woman's mouth) have not thus far been shown to depend on psychopathological conditions. These horrible sexual acts seem

In pre-Christian times, hardly a word was spoken against oral sex

to be committed only by sensual men who have become satiated or impotent from excessive indulgence in a normal way.

So how many of our youthful population have become thus satiated? According to Haas (1979), roughly one in three of the 15–16-year-olds and around half of those aged 17–18 in his southern Californian sample had either given or received oral-genital stimulation. Interestingly, about the same proportions had given oral sex as had received it, from which we may deduce that there are not a large number of people going round with their mouths agape, ever ready to perform oral sex on large numbers of friends and acquaintances and imbalancing the statistics.

What is interesting, however, is that all surveys seem to record a significantly higher percentage of males receiving fellatio than females administering it, whereas most recent surveys indicate that more males than females have taken part in cunnilingus (see table below).

Study	Year	Sex-act	% M	% F
Kinsey	1948 & 1953	cunnilingus	8	14
Haas[1]	1979	cunnilingus	31	34
Haas[2]	1979	cunnilingus	56	59
Delamater	1981	cunnilingus	43	36
Young	1980	cunnilingus	51	31
Newcomer	1985	cunnilingus	50	41
Kinsey	1948 & 1953	fellatio	23	12
Haas[1]	1979	fellatio	33	31
Haas[2]	1979	fellatio	54	41
Delamater	1981	fellatio	41	32
Young	1980	fellatio	58	31
Newcomer	1985	fellatio	44	32

Haas[1] refers to a study on 15–16-year-olds
Haas[2] refers to a study on 17–18-year-olds

The discrepancies between Kinsey and later researchers certainly suggests that at some time between the 1950s and the late 1970s, oral sex became considerably more popular. The recent figures, however, suggest that whereas 41 per cent of 17–18-year-old girls have practised fellatio in 1979, within two years many of them had given it up, leaving a relatively stable figure of 31–2 per cent in all later studies. Indeed, in 1980 fewer women were fellating more men, though this seems to have been an exceptionally good year for men.

In parallel to this, it is remarkable to see the figures for cunnilinguists in the same year when 51 per cent of men were avidly performing oral sex on 31 per cent of women. Never in the field of human concupiscence have so few been licked by so many. Fortunately, by 1985 it is clear that the men were being more generous with their cunnilinguistic abilities.

Another interesting aspect is the surge in cunnilingus from being distinctly rarer than fellatio in the Kinsey study to becoming the more popular of the activities in the latest research. For both males and females, it is now the case that any individual is more likely to have participated in cunnilingus than fellatio. Discussing this phenomenon, Newcomer and Udry relate it to interview material that reveals certain predilections:

> A minority of the boys liked giving oral-genital stimulation and . . . only a minority of the girls reported enjoying it. However, a majority of the boys liked receiving oral-genital stimulation, though only a minority of the girls liked performing fellatio, and then 'only because he wants it' . . . For the boys there seems to be a complex rationale of doing what you don't like in order to receive what you do like, and for the girls, allowing something that you don't like in order to receive something that you might not like anyway; that is, agreeing to cunnilingus, a behavior that maintains 'technical virginity' and does not cause pregnancy, rather than having intercourse.

But who are the fellatrices and cunnilinguists and who are the recipients? Do they do it instead of having intercourse or in addition? These questions were tackled by Newcomer and Udry (1985) by correlating oral sex experience with virginity or the lack thereof.

The following table summarizes their findings.

Activity	M. virgin	M. non-virgin	F. virgin	F. non-virgin
No oral sex	76	19	84	14
Cunnilingus only	10	8	7	16
Fellatio only	2	5	2	2
Cunnilingus and fellatio	12	69	7	69

That the figure 69 should turn up as the percentages of both male and female non-virgins who had performed both fellatio and cunnilingus appears to be totally fortuitous.

In terms of who is doing what to whom, the study revealed that:

> Boys are more likely to have had intercourse than to have given oral-genital stimulation and are more likely to have given oral-genital stimulation than to have received it. Girls are as likely to have received oral-genital stimulation as to have had intercourse and are more likely to have done either than to have given oral-genital stimulation to a boy.

After taking into account the higher likelihood of boys having had intercourse, they concluded: '*Statistically, there is no difference in the order in which boys and girls engage in giving and receiving oral sex, and . . . for girls, cunnilingus occurs no more often than does sexual intercourse.*'

Oddly, although the incidence of oral sex has been greatly studied, its direct effects appear to have elicited less interest. This is a startling omission in view of the important result of Allardyce (1984) who showed that female rats are less likely to become pregnant if they eat the sperm of male rats. In fact, rat sperm ingested by the female leads to the formation of a substance, IgA, in the genital fluid of the female which brings about a reduction in the incidence of pregnancy.

This would appear to add strength to the earlier comment about oral sex not causing pregnancy. If the rats are anything to go by, it could even make it less likely.

Finally we should like to draw attention to Liss-Levinson (1988) which investigates possible connections between disorders of eating and disorders of sexuality. Since oral sex is the natural interface between these two disciplines, it should provide a useful testing ground for any theories. Unfortunately, the research restricts itself to exploring the metaphors used by women with each type of disorder, so cannot really be expected to provide any reliably profound insights in directions relevant to our interest.

References and further reading

Allardyce, R.A. (1984): 'Effect of ingested sperm on fecundity in rats'. *J. Exp. Med.* (159) 1548–53.

Delamater, J. and MacCorquodale, P. (1979): *Premarital Sexuality*. Univ. of Wisconsin Press, Madison.

Haas, W. (1979): *Teenage Sexuality*. Macmillan, NY.

Liss-Levinson, N. (1988): 'Disorders of desire: Women, sex and food'. *Women and Therapy* (7) 121–9.

Kinsey, A.C., Pomeroy, W.B. and Martin, C.E. (1953): *Sexual Behavior in the Human Female*. W.B. Saunders, Philadelphia.

Krafft-Ebing, R. von (1886): *Psychopathia Sexualis*.

Newcomer, S.F. and Udry, J.R. (1985): 'Oral sex in an adolescent population'. *Archives of Sexual Behav.* (14) 1985.

Shostak, A. (1981): 'Oral sex: New standard of intimacy and

old index of troubled sexuality'. *Deviant Behavior: An Interdisciplinary Journal* (2) 127–44.

Young, M. (1980): 'Attitudes and behavior of college students related to oral-genital sexuality'. *Archives of Sexual Behav.* (9) 61–7.

10

Read All About It

When researching possible illustrations for the present volume, the author was caused not inconsiderable embarrassment in various second-hand bookshops in the Soho area of London. Almost without exception, the shop owners, when asked if they stocked any illustrated Victorian erotica, responded with high-minded sneers of ill-disguised disapproval. And when it was explained that the pictures were needed in connection with a forthcoming work of considerable academic respectability, the suspicious glances grew even more marked.

We must therefore hold in the highest regard the valour of Charles Winick who, for the purposes of the research that led to his publication of Winick (1984) and Winick (1985), had to examine all 430 magazines that were offered for sale at an adult bookstore in the Times Square area of New York City.

What he was seeking was a taxonomy of dirty magazines, a means of categorizing their contents into distinct themes. Although shops themselves tended to arrange their material into interest areas, he found their classification to be too coarse for his purposes, so developed a more refined system.

Once this was in place, he could proceed to classify all the magazines, each allocated to a single category according to its dominant theme. Fortunately, the publishers often aided him in the task:

In this adult bookstore, as in many similar stores, patrons are not encouraged to riffle leisurely through the pages of the magazines. Indeed, many magazines are wrapped in cellophane or other coverings and cannot be studied before purchase. Consumers' inability to inspect the magazines may be one reason that many titles more or less clearly communicate the magazines' content (e.g. *Painful Pleasures, Oreo Sex, B and D Review, Mother Suckers, Bald Beavers, Lesbian Girls, Big Titters, Swingers' Update*). Other well-known series, with more heterogeneous content, have titles with fewer denotations (e.g., *Puritan, Flair, Swedish Erotica, Hot, Eros, Private*). It appears that many consumers know what to expect in terms of a specific magazine's content.

By classifying each magazine and taking into account the number of its pages, Winick was able to assess the relative proportions of material corresponding to his various categories. Here, then, are the 1985 top twenty for themes in pornographic magazines:

1	Women in various degrees of undress	27.8%
2	Male–female non-explicit sexual activity	15.5%
3	Male–female explicit sexual activity	8.4%
4	Bondage and Discipline (sexual interaction with a person who is tied up)*	4.9%
5	Oral-genital heterosexual activity	2.9%
6	Special sexual activity (e.g. involving dildos or urination)	2.8%
7	Women's body-parts (breasts, buttocks or legs)	2.7%
8	Lesbian	2.6%
9	Swingers (partner-swapping including addresses)	1.9%

*In 85 per cent of the Bondage-Discipline magazines, there was a clearly unequal power relationship between males and females. Of these, males were dominant in 71 per cent and submissive in 29 per cent.

10	Young women (but always carrying the legend that all the models are over-18)	1.9%
11	Special Groups of Women (e.g., blondes or genitally shaven)	1.4%
12	Interracial (heterosexual black and white)	1.4%
13	Homosexual male	1.3%
14	Sado-Masochism	1.2%
15	Ethnic (non-white women)	1.2%
16	Fetishistic (e.g. boots or rubber)	1.1%
17	Group Sex	1.1%
18	Nudism (in naturalistic settings)	1.0%
19	Anal (heterosexual anal intercourse)	1.0%
20	Women wrestling	1.0%

Bondage and Discipline

83.1 per cent of all material fell into the above categories, with the remainder classified either as 'Mixed' (no single category dominant) or 'Other' (any other category totally less than 1 per cent).

It was estimated that over 80 per cent of the persons shown in the magazines were in their twenties, with only 1 per cent over forty. The degree of their physical attractiveness, however, varied greatly.

> By and large, the persons shown appear to be middle class. Many of the men are shown working at occupations which bring them into homes (e.g. appliance repair). About half the people shown appear to be married. Conversation and dialogue in the fiction in these magazines tend to be simple and explicit.

The author reaches no clear conclusions about why people buy these magazines, though interviews with the owners of the stores do confirm that the amount of space allocated to each magazine tends to be in direct proportion to its popularity.

> It would be necessary to interview the customers of the bookshops in order to determine the functions served by these magazines. We can speculate that their male readers may be obtaining information, exercising fantasies, obtaining reassurance, collecting and comparing materials, seeking stimulation and obtaining guidance in overcoming sexual difficulties, among other reasons.

Sadly, this further research appears not yet to have been carried out. It is interesting to speculate what responses one might get from frequenters of adult bookstores, if they were given questionnaires asking them to list the categories of material they had a) browsed and b) purchased, and to assess whether the function they expect the magazine to serve is (on a seven-point scale ranging from 'not at all' to 'exclusively') information-obtaining, fantasy-exercising, reassuring, collecting and comparing, stimulating or therapeutic.

The author does, however, envisage replicating the study in several years' time in the expectation that 'tracking the content of sexually explicit magazines over time can permit some correlation between changes in their content and changes in the larger society.'

A highly specific study on the effects and appeal of the Bondage–Discipline category was done by Heilbrun and Seif (1988), who showed pictures of female models in bondage to 54 young-adult males. By comparing reported levels of arousal with apparent distress levels of the models, and with personality attributes of the subjects, some important conclusions could be drawn.

Firstly, they found that pictures of a distressed model in bondage were viewed as more exciting than pictures of the same model apparently enjoying herself ('displaying positive affect').

Secondly, they discovered that the degree to which subjects found distressed models in bondage exciting, depended on their scores on a measure of anti-social tendencies and on their abilities to recognize emotions as expressed in facial expressions (facial-decoding).

'The erotic value of distressed females in bondage was greatest when subjects combined greater anti-sociality and better facial-decoding skill.'

In other words, sadism is more likely to turn you on if you are anti-social and can recognize when someone is in pain.

The above studies were limited to rather specialist tastes in sexual material. Abramson and Mechanic (1983) attempted a far more general approach, categorizing incidences of sex in bestselling novels and popular films over three decades. Whereas magazines in adult shops might be taken as a reflection of the needs of their customers, popular novels and films, particularly the smutty ones, also serve an educative purpose, acting as a major source of

Specialist tastes in sexual material

information on sexual topics.

Books and films with mass-market appeal, therefore, might be expected not only to reflect changes in society's values, but also to some extent to lead them.

With all that in mind, they proceeded to watch the most successful films (in terms of box-office receipts) and read the bestselling works of fiction, looking for sex scenes to classify and compare.

So, after reading a selection that ranged from *Doctor Zhivago*, *Lolita* and *Lady Chatterley's Lover* to *Scruples* and *The World According to Garp*, and watching a selection from *Some Like It Hot* and *The Love Bug* to *Alien* and *The Amityville Horror*, they set about recording who did what to whom and why, according to a pre-designed classification scheme.

Specifically, the 29 scoring categories (there were originally 48, but they refined them) were: initiation of sexual action, attractiveness, conquest mentality, age, length of time acquainted, marital status, adultery, physical health, occupation, setting, erotic details, romantic love, eroticism, description of genitalia, description of orgasm, sexual satisfaction, degree of communication (before, during and after sex), use of intoxicants, use of contraceptives, incest, non-heterosexual sex, masturbation, sex during menstruation, use of lubricant, sexual dysfunction, sexual aggressiveness, lack of sexual desire, status gain and monetary gain.

Two females and three males took part in the experiment, rating pre-selected passages on the above categories. In order, presumably, to save their time, one of the experimenters had read all the books and selected five sexual passages from each ('or where five did not exist, all passages were used'). The rater thus had to read only the dirty bits, though page numbers were also supplied where valuable additional background material might be found. They watched the films all the way through and rated all the sexual encounters.

What was interesting was firstly the differences found when materials from 1959, 1969 and 1979 were compared, and secondly some aspects which remained constant throughout the period.

An analysis of the sex passages in books revealed significant changes in five of the scoring categories across the three decades:

1 *Length of time acquainted* Whereas in the most popular books of 1959, 50 per cent of sexual partners would have known each other a year and 27.3 per cent would have known each other for between one and five years, before they jumped into bed together, by 1969 these figures had dropped to 7.5 per cent (1 year courtship) and 10 per cent (long courtship).
2 *Romantic love* In 1959, a moderate amount of caring was shown by 50 per cent of fictional sex-partners, with 22.7 per cent showing a high amount of romantic caring and only 10.6 per cent not caring at all. Twenty years later, it was 35.4 per cent moderate caring, 4.2 per cent high caring and as many as 45.8 per cent not caring at all.
3 *Male marital status* In 1979, single men did 79.2 per cent of the love-making, with divorced men making no contribution at all. This is a decisive shift from the figures of earlier decades which were 54.5 per cent single, 18.2 per cent divorced in 1959, and 55 per cent single, 12.5 per cent divorced in 1969.
4 *Communication during sex* They don't talk about it any more. In 1959 and 1969, there was always some communication, either verbal or non-verbal, during intercourse. They always talked, murmured, purred or

found some other way to communicate. But in 1979, as many as 10.4 per cent of fictional mating couples were assessed as having no communication whatsoever.

5 *Post-coital communication* And it's just as bad afterwards. Not communicating after sex went up from 9.1 per cent in 1959 and 10 per cent in 1969 to a massive 45.8 per cent in 1979.

In summary, then, the modern bedmates of literary fiction have known each other for less than a year, the man is single, they don't care for each other and they just get on with the sex without talking either during or afterwards.

Additionally, it is worth mentioning that across all the years nearly 80 per cent of the women and 63 per cent of the men were described as attractive, and over 95 per cent of both were in good health. The orgasm count favoured men, with their orgasms mentioned in 69.1 per cent of the acts, while the comparable figure for women was 49.1 per cent. When orgasm was mentioned for women, it was described as 'incredible' in 31.8 per cent of cases with 'pleasurable' a poor runner-up on 11.8 per cent. Sex for monetary gain was very rare (7.3 per cent male, 8.2 per cent female), neither was there much indication of incest, masturbation, lubricants, contraceptives or intoxicants. But there was quite a lot of 'sexy lingerie' (16.4 per cent).

The most common sexual dysfunctions were non-orgasmic women (8.3 per cent), flaccid men (6.4 per cent) and premature ejaculation (5.5 per cent). Whenever a penis was described, however, it was almost always 'large'. Women's breasts, buttocks or vaginas came in various sizes.

In films, there are similar trends, though partners do tend to jump into bed after only a few days' acquaintance and many of the men are older than in the books. Oddly, post-marital sex was entirely absent in the films viewed from 1959 and 1969, where in 1979 half the sex-participants were married (but not necessarily to the person they were having sex with). They did, however, whether married or not, tend to talk much more both during and after sex, though no one mentioned orgasm.

The comparatively weak results from films as compared with novels may be due to the set of ethical guidelines which have always governed the industry. The production code produced by the Hays Office in 1934 included the following injunctions:

> excessive and lustful kissing, lustful embraces, suggestive postures and gestures, are not to be shown; miscegenation is forbidden; sex hygiene and venereal diseases are not subjects for motion pictures; illicit sex is contrary to divine law and in a number of cases contrary to human law; because of the natural and spontaneous reaction of normal human beings to sexual stimuli, the portrayal of definite manifestations of sex is harmful to individual morality, subversive to the interests of society and a peril to the human race.

All of which may help to explain why, in the films selected for 1959, there were only two scorable sex scenes, and Doris Day was in one of them and Tony Curtis dressed up as a woman for most of the other.

Here are some of the conclusions reached by Abramson and Mechanic based on the above findings:

> While the results do not imply that there is currently a void of long-term sexually romantic relationships in best-selling fiction, they do indicate that superficial sexual relationships are now more prevalent . . .
>
> Where male attractiveness is concerned, men are now being described as physically attractive, whereas in earlier fiction they were more likely to have been described as 'average looking' . . .
>
> Finally, the characterizations of sexual participants as single and attractive have comparable negative consequences. First, given that a large percentage of sexually active couples are married, it gives the distorted perception

that sexual activity is the sole province of single people. This is a very unfortunate circumstance, since pleasurable sexual relations are integral to marital satisfaction. Also, there are no data to suggest that attractive people are more sexually active, functional, or competent.

And finally: *'It is obvious from this study, that the success of a book or movie is certainly not dependent on its sexual content.'*

Before leaving the subject of sex in magazines, books and films, we should comment briefly on an area we have not yet browsed: that of the popular erotica usually referred to as soft porn.

Kenrick, Gutierres and Goldberg (1989) studied the effects on people of looking at centrefold pictures of naked women. Specifically, they wanted to find out whether looking at pictures of naked women affected later assessments of how attractive they found somebody else to be.

So in their first experiment, 107 male and 89 female subjects were asked to judge the attractiveness of a female in a nude photograph. For the purposes of the experiment, one group of subjects had previously been looking at abstract

'There are no data to suggest that attractive people are more sexually active'

art, a second group had been viewing 'average nudes', while the third group had been looking at photographs from erotic magazines.

The result was that both male and female subjects were inclined to judge the naked woman as less attractive if they had first been looking at the centrefolds.

In their second experiment, 35 male and 35 female subjects all looked at erotic pictures before making their judgements, but the men looked at pictures of naked women, while the women looked at pictures of naked men. In this case, it was only the men who were liable to judge the original nude as less attractive than they would have had they not just been looking at dirty pictures.

A sad by-product of this research was the finding that: '*Males who found the* Playboy *type centrefolds more pleasant rated themselves as less in love with their wives.*'

Finally, we must consider the question of whether pornography can damage the health, or at least to what extent people believe that it might. Merritt, Gerstl and LoSciuto (1975) analysed the results of a nation-wide American survey of the attitudes of 2,486 adults to erotica-pornography. The respondents were given twelve sentences, each of which described a possible effect of pornography. For each item, they had to say whether they believed it had that effect, and if it did, whether it had had that effect on the respondent or someone he or she knew personally. Here are the twelve items:

1 Sexual materials provide entertainment.
2 Sexual materials make people bored with sexual materials.
3 Sexual materials provide an outlet for bottled-up impulses.
4 Sexual materials make people sex crazy.
5 Sexual materials give relief to people who have sex problems.
6 Sexual materials lead to a breakdown of morals.

7 Sexual materials improve sex relations of some married couples.
8 Sexual materials provide information about sex.
9 Sexual materials excite people sexually.
10 Sexual materials lead people to commit rape.
11 Sexual materials lead people to lose respect for women.
12 Sexual materials make men want to do new things with their wives.

Interestingly, while 67 per cent of the respondents believed that sexual materials excite people sexually, only 22 per cent had been sexually excited themselves by them. And nobody admitted to having been driven sex crazy or to have committed a rape through exposure to sexual materials.

The main point of the research was to discover whether people attributed positive effects (items 1, 3, 5, 7 and 8), negative effects (4, 6, 10 and 11) or neutral effects (2, 9 and 12) to pornography. As expected, women took a markedly more negative view on the matter than did men, but the other strong result was that negative attitudes increased with age. While younger people stressed the positive aspects, the older men became the more they felt that the effects of pornography were bad.

> These results as such are unable to confirm any specific notions about *why* the age factor should be so pervasive in its effects. Do attitudes about erotica change as individuals age, or are we witnessing a 'generational' (historical cohort) difference?

An interesting question. But whatever the answer, this piece of research seems to suggest that the traditional idea of a 'dirty old man' is the exception rather than the rule.

In a related piece of research, incidentally, Griffith and Walker (1975) showed that a woman's reactions to erotic slides do not depend on what point she is at in her menstrual cycle.

References and further reading

Abramson, P.R. and Mechanic, M.B. (1983): 'Sex and the media: Three decades of best-selling books and major motion pictures'. *Archives of Sexual Behav.* (12) 185–206.

Griffith, M. and Walker, C.E. (1975): 'Menstrual cycle phases and personality variables as related to response to erotic stimuli'. *Archives of Sexual Behav.* (4) 599–603.

Haring, M. and Meyerson, L. (1979): 'Attitudes of college students toward sexual behavior of disabled persons'. *Arch. Phys. Med. Rehab.* (60) 257–60.

Heilbrun Jr, A.B. and Seif, D.T. (1988): 'Erotic value of female distress in sexually explicit photographs'. *J. Sex Research* (24) 47–57.

Kenrick, D.T., Gutierres, S.E. and Goldberg, L.L. (1989): 'Influence of popular erotica on judgments of strangers and mates'. *J. Exp. Soc. Psychology* (25) 159–67.

Malamuth, N. and Spinner, B. (1980): 'A longitudinal content analysis of sexual violence in the best-selling erotic magazines'. *J. Sex Research* (16) 226–37.

Merritt, C.G., Gerstl, J.E. and LoSciuto, L.A. (1975): 'Age and perceived sample effects of erotica-pornography: A national sample study'. *Archives of Sexual Behav.* (4) 605–21.

Smith, D.C. (1976): 'The social content of pornography'. *Journal of Communication* (26) 16–24.

Winick, C. (1984): 'Licit sex industries and services'. In Boggs, V., Handel, G. and Fava, S. (Eds), *The Apple Sliced: Sociological Studies of New York City*. Praeger, NY.

Winick, C. (1985): 'A content analysis of sexually explicit magazines sold in an adult bookshop'. *J. Sex Research* (21) 206–10.

11

With Legs Spread Wide in Stirrups

The role of sexual fantasies in erotic arousal is something that impinges deeply on any psychoanalytic approach to sexual functioning. Fantasy in general is adopted as a defence mechanism against conflicts, but, as Crepault, Abraham, Porto and Couture (1978) point out, sexual fantasies seem to play a more positive role.

> Erotic fantasy is capable of adapting itself to compensate for the insufficiency of external or personal reality. It plays a feedback part by correcting sexual activity as the latter unfurls. Thus, an inclination towards fantasmic activity is noted especially when sexual relations with a partner are of long duration or frequency.

In other words, if sex goes on for too long, you get bored with whatever is, or more likely is not, going on and compensate by fantasizing.

> However, erotic fantasies may also be considered not only as a compensatory phenomenon but also as a sort of erotic enrichment, more all-embracing than the erogenous possibilities of the subject. This would lead to the notion that, even though it occasionally betrays symptoms of neurosis or pervert pathological tendencies, erotic fantasy is usually described as a normal occurrence and the possibility of using the imaginary in the process of

excitation, without allowing it to become an indispensable element of sexual health, would confirm a sexual and psychoaffective state of well-being.

In other words, if you are not stimulated enough by your partner, fantasy can be good for your emotional health. Indeed, fantasy is so normal and healthy, that they consider it may occupy an 'intrapsychic erogenic zone and in some ways be considered an authentic mechanism of erogeneity'.

The acceptance of fantasizing as an indispensable part of sexual health led the researchers to ask certain questions:

Are men's fantasies the same as women's?

Is there a difference between fantasies in the early stage of sex and those in the run-up to orgasm?

Would fantasies persist in the course of an ideal sexual experience, where every erotic desire is fulfilled?

As a small step towards approaching these important questions, Crepault, Abraham, Porto and Couture asked 66 women (aged 20–40) from three different countries to describe their sexual fantasies. ('We have limited our enquiries to female subjects as they are more readily inclined to describe their erotic fantasies.' The researchers were all male, incidentally.) They interviewed them; they gave them a questionnaire; they asked them to keep diaries.

In the questionnaire, the subjects were given a list of 31 fantasies, and asked which they had experienced during sexual activity with their usual partner, assessing each as 'often', 'occasionally' or 'never'. Then they had to do the same thing relating to fantasies while masturbating.

Finally, they kept records of sexual activity and fantasies in a month-long diary, then filled in another questionnaire concerning their orgasmic experiences.

Here is the fantasy checklist, with percentage responses:

Description of fantasy scene	*often*	*occasionally*	*never*
1 Scene reviving a former sexual encounter	25.8	53.0	21.2
2 With a different sexual partner	19.7	59.1	21.2
3 Scene from a sexually exciting movie	16.7	54.5	28.8
4 You embrace male genitals	33.3	30.3	36.4
5 A man embraces your genitals	24.2	39.4	36.4
6 A romantic scene	24.2	36.4	39.4
7 A seducer excites you sexually	15.1	39.4	45.5
8 You are the sex object of several men	21.2	28.8	50.0
9 You witness the sexual performance of other persons	13.6	36.4	50.0
10 You are tied up while being sexually stimulated by a man	22.7	25.8	51.5
11 An enormous penis penetrates you	15.1	27.3	57.6
12 You witness group sex activities	13.6	28.8	57.6
13 You are a victim of aggression	9.1	33.3	57.6
14 You pretend to struggle and resist before succumbing to a man's sexual advances	12.1	27.3	60.6
15 You find yourself with an imaginary lover	7.6	31.8	60.6
16 You are observed during sex	3.1	34.8	62.1
17 You have sex with another woman	7.6	27.3	65.1
18 You receive male ejaculation in your mouth	13.6	19.7	66.7
19 You receive anal penetration	12.1	19.7	68.2
20 You see yourself with another body	7.6	22.7	69.7
21 You see yourself as a prostitute	7.6	22.7	69.7
22 You are being fondled by a faceless lover	4.5	24.2	71.3
23 Your sexual activities are performed in public	4.5	22.7	72.8
24 You yourself are the aggressor	4.5	22.7	72.8
25 You are overpowered and forced to have sex with one or more strangers	4.5	18.2	77.3

Description of fantasy scene	often	occasionally	never
26 You are obliged to have sex against your will with someone you know	3.0	16.7	80.3
27 You initiate a boy in sexual functions	6.1	12.1	81.8
28 You perform actions considered dirty or forbidden	1.5	16.7	81.8
29 You are the object of humiliation	1.5	13.6	84.9
30 You receive a beating	1.5	12.1	86.4
31 You are the sexual partner of an animal	1.5	9.1	89.4

An immediate and obvious conclusion to be drawn from these figures is that the women in the sample did indeed

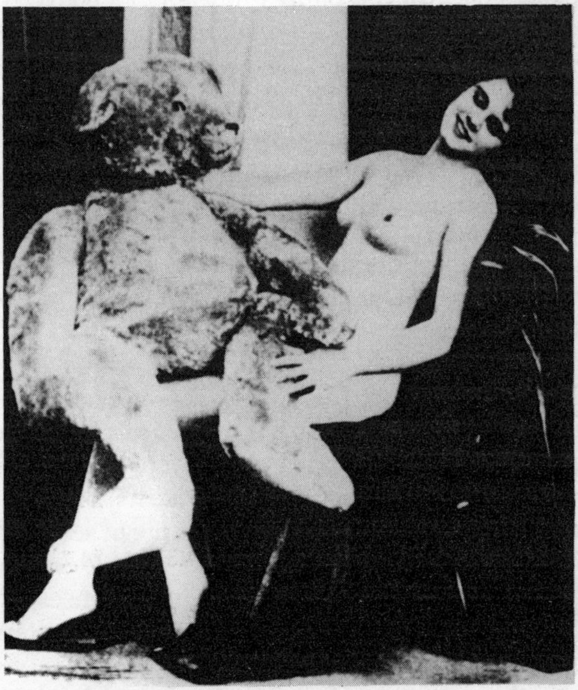

'You are the sexual partner of an animal'

have a large number of sexual fantasies, in complete contrast to the findings of Hessellund (1976) whose results reported only 8 per cent of women as having erotic fantasies during heterosexual activity.

However, the above findings are in line with Hollender (1963 and 1970) and Fisher (1973) who agree on 75 per cent as the likely figure. Fisher's women do, however, appear to have some fantasies that are not immediately identified with the 31 above:

'I think of myself in a hospital bed . . . my legs spread wide in stirrups.'

'I used to imagine stories about girls who nursed and aided injured men who later fell in love with the girls.'

'I was floating over an expansive field of flowers.'

'A picture of husband and self combined into one person.'

Anyway, back to the figures in the table above. It was further recorded that 13.6 per cent of the sample always fantasized while having sex, 39.4 per cent often did so and 40.9 per cent rarely did. The most common time for erotic fantasies to appear was 'immediately prior to the pre-orgasmic phase' of activities. They were also quite popular during the excitatory phase until the onset of orgasm, but none of the subjects had fantasies during orgasm itself 'which may indicate an antithesis existing between imagination and the orgasmic explosion'. And it made no significant difference whether they came from Quebec, France or Switzerland.

Indeed, even when the content of the fantasies was analysed, there was a remarkably high degree of similarity between countries. Only on one item were there significant differences, which was that Quebec women more frequently fantasized about being 'the object of desire in several men'.

The really interesting stage of the research came when factor analysis was applied to the responses to the questionnaire. What this does is to detect patterns of response and establish linkages between groups of items to reveal the underlying trends behind an individual's set of answers. And what they found was that there were six principal factors of fantasy:

Factor 1: Being the aggressor; being the victim of aggression; being a prostitute; having sex against one's will; struggling before submitting.

Factor 2: Romantic; embracing man's genitals; having one's own genitals embraced; being tied up and stimulated.

Factor 3: Group sex; having sex with another man; being the sex object of several men; seeing oneself with another body.

Factor 4: Initiating a boy; being penetrated by an enormous penis; being excited by a seducer.

Factor 5: Receiving a beating; receiving ejaculation in one's mouth; being humiliated.

Factor 6: Witnessing sexual performance of others; performing in public.

The explanations given for these factors are as follows:

Factor 1 involves denial of responsibility for sexual

Factor 5: Receiving a beating

enjoyment, either by masochistic fantasy or by a change of image that absolves the fantasizer of guilt.

Factor 2 is a dialectical fantasy confronting the personalization of romance with the depersonalization of the body as sex object.

Factor 3 is simply narcissistic, while Factor 4 confirms a need for confirmation of adult status.

Factor 5 is moral masochism and Factor 6 implies a need to confirm one's physical image.

In explaining the often insubstantial and confused nature of these assessments, the researchers say: '*We are aware of our limitations and of the condensed character of the interpretations suggested and we know they are provisional analyses which should be further amplified.*'

A single score was also obtained for each woman on the questionnaire, counting 1, 2 or 3 respectively for each item marked 'never', 'occasionally' or 'often'. The 31 items thus gave a possible range between 31 and 93 points. Total scores were then compared with biographical and other data, and the following conclusions were reached:

The women who indulge most in erotic fantasies while making love are better educated than those who fantasize less. The high fantasizers are also likely to have started masturbating at an earlier age, to have indulged in sex games (both hetero and homosexual) during early childhood, to masturbate at least once a week, to reach orgasm through masturbation more quickly and to like both vaginal and clitoral stimulation.

On the subject of male fantasies, we refer the reader to the excellent work of Smith and Over, already discussed in chapter 4.

Further details about both male and female fantasies were obtained by Gold and Chick (1988) who gave questionnaires to 79 female and 81 male undergraduates and asked them to write about three of their commonly occurring sexual fantasies.

Their objective was to measure attitudes, sexual experience and guilt by means of the questionnaires and see how they correlated with explicitness, length and emotionality of fantasies. What they discovered was that liberal attitudes were associated with longer, more explicit fantasies (or at least with the willingness to write longer and more explicit accounts of their fantasies), and that more sexual experience was associated with longer, more explicit and more emotional fantasies.

The statistical technique of stepwise regression suggested that sexual experience was the best overall predictor of sexual fantasies.

Finally, as a footnote to the earlier mention of similarities between the fantasies of women from Quebec, France and Switzerland, this might be an appropriate place to discuss Earls and Proulx (1986). This research involved playing sound tapes to ten French-speaking Canadian rapists and ten French-speaking non-rapists. The audio materials all represented forms of sexual behaviour, corresponding to four categories: mutually consenting, rape, aggressive and sexually neutral. All the subjects wore penile tumescence gauges while listening to the tapes.

There was no difference between rapists and non-rapists when listening to the mutually consenting sexual tapes, but there was a significant difference for rape (with rapists, as predicted, showing higher levels of arousal), which became still more marked when the tapes were analysed using a rape index. Since similar results had been obtained on English-speaking rapists, a clear conclusion was drawn: *'It is suggested that the identification of rapists using penile tumescence may be independent of both language and culture.'*

References and further reading

Arndt, W.B., Foehl, J.C. and Good, F.E. (1985): 'Specific sexual fantasy themes: A multidimensional study'. *J. Pers. Soc. Psychol.*(48) 472–8.

Crepault, C., Abraham, G., Porto, R. and Couture, M. (1976): 'Erotic Imagery in Women'. In *Progress in Sexology* (Ed. R. Gemme), Plenum Press.

Crepault, C. and Couture, M. (1980): 'Men's erotic fantasies'. *Archives of Sexual Behav.* (9) 565–81.

Earls, C.M. and Proulx, J. (1986): 'The differentiation of Francophone rapists and non-rapists using penile circumference measures'. *Criminal Justice and Behavior* (13) 414–29.

Fisher, S. (1973): *Understanding the Female Orgasm.* Penguin Books.

Gold, S.R. and Chick, D.A. (1988): 'Sexual fantasy patterns as related to sexual attitude, experience, guilt and sex'. *J. Sex Education and Therapy* (14) 18–23.

Hariton, E.B. and Singer, J.L. (1974): 'Women's fantasies during sexual intercourse: Normative and theoretical implications'. *J. Consult. Clin. Psychology* (42) 313–22.

Hessellund, H. (1976): 'Masturbation and sexual fantasies in married couples'. *Archives of Sexual Behav.* (5) 133–47.

Hollender, M.H. (1963): 'Women's fantasies during sexual intercourse'. *Archives of General Psychiatry* (8) 86–90.

Hollender, M.H. (1970): 'Women's coital fantasies'. *Medical Aspects of Human Sexuality* (4) 63–70.

Smith, D. and Over, R. (1987): 'Correlates of fantasy-induced and film-induced male sexual arousal'. *Archives of Sexual Behav.* (16) 395–409.

Wilson, G.D. (1988): 'Measurement of sex fantasy'. *J. Sexual and Marital Ther.* (3) 45–55.

12

Sex, Drugs & Rock 'n' Roll

'Investigators have long been interested in the relationship between androgen levels and sexual activity in the human male', wrote Kraemer, Becker, Brodie, Doering, Moos and Hamburg in 1976, and most of that interest has been centred on the male hormone testosterone.

Testosterone is produced in the testes, and is responsible for the development of the primary sex organs and secondary characteristics such as facial hair. It has also been shown that administration of testosterone to treat some forms of hormone deficiency has the side effect of increasing libido. Also drugs that interfere with the action of testosterone have been shown to reduce both libido and potency.

So does this mean that men with an active sex life have higher natural testosterone levels than those with comparatively inactive ones? The answer to that question turns out to be much more complex than it might appear.

Fox, Ismail, Love, Kirkham and Loraine (1972) did tests on a remarkably cooperative subject to report that testosterone levels were significantly higher during and immediately after sexual intercourse as compared with levels when resting. But Lee, Jaffe and Midgley (1974) tested five subjects 23 and 24 hours before intercourse then 10 minutes, 30 minutes, 1½ hours, 24 hours and 48 hours after intercourse, and found no significant changes in testosterone levels over time.

Pirke, Kockott and Dittmar (1974) preferred not to disturb their subjects so soon after sex, so avoided post-coitus interruptus by showing them sexually explicit films instead and measuring their testosterone levels before, during and after. They found that blue movies did increase testosterone levels, and that they reached a peak 60–90 minutes after the film had ended.

What made their study more intriguing, however, was a parallel investigation, correlating testosterone levels with weekly orgasm frequencies among a group of eight young males. What they found there was that the men who enjoyed the *most* orgasms tended to have *lower* levels of testosterone.

So Doering et al (1974) decided to get to the bottom of the matter by paying 20 normal heterosexual males to give blood samples every other day for two months, always at 8.00 a.m., while also keeping a record of their sexual activity. All they had to do was note on each day of the study the number of times they had intercourse, masturbated or performed any other sexual activity to achieve orgasm.

Testosterone levels in each blood sample were then measured and the results separated according to whether the sample came from 'a period with orgasmic activity'. (For the purposes of the study, this definition depended on whether or not there was an orgasm between 32 hours before the testing and 16 hours after.)

For one subject, every day was an orgasmic day; for another the proportion of orgasmic to non-orgasmic days was only 0.091. There were also considerable variations in testosterone levels, both between individuals and on different days for the same individual.

The results showed significantly higher levels of testosterone following a period in which orgasm had occurred. When levels were compared on days before orgasm and days before non-orgasm, no differences were found. The conclusion was therefore reached that high testosterone levels are 'more likely a consequence than a precursor of sexual activity'.

But there was a significant negative correlation between mean testosterone levels of individuals and their orgasm frequency.

'This indicates that the more sexually active the man, the lower his average testosterone level tends to be.'

So, a summary of the whole research produces the paradox that if Mr A has sex once a week, he will probably have a higher testosterone level than Mr B, who has sex every day; but if Mr A then increases his sexual activity to the level of Mr B's, his testosterone level will shoot even further up, rather than coming down to Mr B's level.

While admitting that 'the structure of the relationship between sexual activity and testosterone cannot here be definitively ascertained', the researchers do produce an interesting theory to explain their figures. Their suggestion is that while sexual activity increases testosterone levels, it could also be true that sexual abstinence reduces it. Once

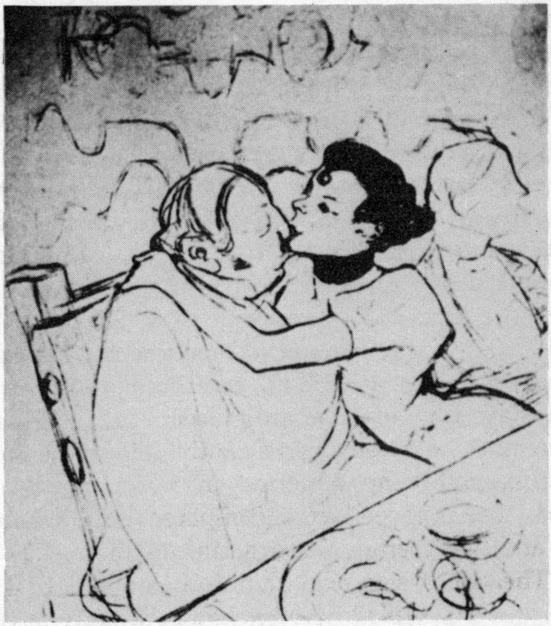

Mr B, who has sex every day

it falls to dangerously low levels, you need to have sex to top it up.

Now for a man with naturally high testosterone levels, this situation would rarely arise, but for someone whose natural levels are low, there could be a frequent need for sex as the critical level is reached more often.

The whole thing is undoubtedly complicated by known effects of testosterone on stress, nervousness and anxiety, all of which could also affect or be affected by sexual abstinence or activity.

Far more research is clearly needed, but before leaving this topic, we should mention Anonymous (1970) who shaved with an electric razor each morning and weighed the hairs collected. His findings showed that beard growth (which is also believed to be stimulated by high testosterone levels) was greatest on days preceding expected sexual activity. The level then stayed high on the next day also. So the anticipation of sex makes your beard grow.

We move on to music.

St Lawrence and Joyner (1991) set out to investigate the effects that listening to sexually violent rock music might have on males' attitudes towards violence against women. Questionnaires were given to male subjects before and after an experimental period during which they were assigned to groups listening to different types of music ranging from heavy metal with violent lyrics via non-violent heavy metal to classical.

They found that 'exposure to heavy metal rock music, irrespective of lyrical content, increased males' sex-role stereotyping and negative attitudes towards women'.

Since they had also asked the subjects to provide subjective assessments of their arousal levels, they were also able to report: *'An unexpected finding was greater self-reported sexual arousal in response to classical music.'*

The finding that lyrical content was irrelevant to effect is not a matter that will be greeted well by song lyricists. But even if lyrics do not affect sexuality, it is clear that sexual attitudes have an effect on song lyrics. Armstrong (1986) investigated the lyric content of country music sex songs. The controversy over the issue that he hoped to tackle was whether the words of such songs reflected the common experience of their predominantly working-class audience, or whether they were just filthy.

He started by assembling a collection of song lyrics that had been produced commercially and played on radio at least once in the fifteen years preceding the study. The next stage was a categorization of sexual themes in the lyrics, which was not as easy as it might seem:

> Often sexual content is difficult to ascertain. Some songs are highly metaphorical. For example, equestrian expressions often connote sexuality. Certainly this applies to two songs, 'I Got The Hoss':
>
> I got the hoss, you got the saddle
> Together we're gonna ride, ride, ride.
>
> and 'Plastic Saddle':
>
> Don't give me no plastic saddle
> I want to feel that leather when I ride
> Don't give me no paint and powder
> Honey let me see the hide.

In view of the problems posed by such metaphorical lyrics, the study was restricted to songs with unambiguous themes. The themes that emerged were the following (with the number of songs representing each theme in brackets): Prostitution (16), Extramarital Sex (15), Illegitimacy (10), Homosexuality (5), Impotency (4), Statutory Rape (3), Masturbation (2), Forcible Rape (2), Infertility (2), Interracial Dating (2), Nymphomania (2), Transvestism (2), Birth Control (1), Frigidity (1), Incest (1), Pornography (1), Voyeurism (1), Zoophilia (1)*.

*The score on Zoophilia should, perhaps, be registered as only ½ since the object of the singer's love was a mermaid.

Since 'cheatin' love' is such a popular theme in country songs, the large category of Extramarital Sex was considerably reduced to a final selection of 15 songs, each representing different reactions by husbands to a wife's infidelity.

Besides these categories, the songs divided into four main areas: Comic and Novelty Songs (where the story and the sex are not meant to be taken seriously), Story Songs (with a clear story-line and usually a direct message), Commentary Songs (criticisms of hypocrisy and expressions of fatalism) and Societal Reaction Songs (where the principal theme is the reaction of society to the sexual issue). A fifth area of Multiple Category Songs (combining more than one of the first four categories) completes the classification.

Whereas many of the original 18 categories seem to fall easily into this new broad classification system (for example, songs about transvestism, pornography, voyeurism or masturbation all seem to fall under Comic and Novelty), the classification of songs about extramarital sex poses a far greater problem owing to the 'vast array of subtopics' in their lyrics.

The researcher accordingly took one particular dimension, that of the husband's reaction, and made a list of the possible behaviours:

1 Go crazy
2 Batter the informant
3 Denial
4 Beg for a denial
5 Say and do nothing
6 Laugh
7 Cheat
8 Get drunk
9 Throw her out of the house, with regrets
10 Throw her out of the house, without regrets
11 Suicide through drug overdose
12 Kill her (by pushing off a cliff)
13 Kill the other man (by shooting him)

The object of the singer's love was a mermaid

14 Kill her and the other man (by stabbing them)
15 Kill her and mutilate the corpse

This last possibility comes in a song entitled 'I'm Gonna Kill You (And Bury You in a Box About Half Your Size)'.

Having got this far, the researcher ended his paper with the conclusion: *'I can find no common factors in these extramarital sex or ''cheating'' songs. The major generalization suggested by these data is to avoid generalization.'*

Moyle (1975), however, has no such problems in dealing with the sexual songs of Samoa. He concludes:

> The Samoan world, which calls for the full exercise of bodily gifts and the satisfaction of bodily needs, does not lose sight of propriety. While acknowledging the license associated with some song texts . . . sexuality, in whatever

premeditated or spontaneous form, is never allowed to develop to the stage of prurience or to transcend existing sanctions against adultery and incest. Far from being completely free in its modes of expression, it adheres to traditional formalized patterns which determine its occasions, participants and verbal and kinetic limits.

These verbal and kinetic limits are well illustrated by the beautiful marriage song '*Le ala i mafa e*', of which the lyrics translate as:

The way into the vagina, the way into the vagina.
The sacred urine vomits out, the sacred urine vomits out.
There was no previous intercourse, there was no previous intercourse.
[Name of groom] is a chief's son, [name of bride] is a titled lady.
First because of the first.

The opening lines are a reference to the act of defloration followed by the resultant spilling of blood. The last line refers again to his being her first man.

The same poetic expressiveness pervades the adolescents' song, '*Tau laga'ali*':

Gather laga'ali leaves, gather laga'ali leaves.
Reach for the vagina, it is agape
Gather moso'oi leaves, gather moso'oi leaves.
Reach for the vagina, it is bleeding.
Stick your finger in and smell it
As if it were something fragrant
The farting thing
Lies next to your arsehole.

We cannot leave Samoa without mentioning their dance, of which Moyle (1975) provides a potent description:

> In all mixed nonsynchronized dancing, the male tries to catch the attention of the female and to distract her; he does this by a variety of means – slapping his arms and chest loudly, making provocative gestures just out of her field of vision, or occasionally displaying his genitalia directly to her . . . A male dancer may approach a girl from behind and stand only one or two inches from her, imitating the mechanics of animal copulation; this is the most overt sexual feature of contemporary dance, but is seen only occasionally, and never lasts for more than a few seconds . . . As sexually explicit dance movements are always considered highly amusing, it might be possible to extend the notion of formalized humor and define such actions as kinetic joking.

But if one is to express the Samoan dancer's sexual exposure within the notion of formalized humour, it would presumably have to fall somewhere in Raskin's (1984) taxonomy of humour, which breaks sexual humour into five areas: Genital Size, Prowess, Sexual Exposure, Sexual Ignorance and Forbidden Sex.

If the Samoan male dancer exposes himself, then his genital size immediately becomes a potential topic for humour in the sexual exposure category, and Raskin points out that variations in size of genital organs form part of everyone's internalized semantic script, i.e. we know what is meant to be funny, or, as he puts it:

> In sexual humour, this information, which is clearly part of the native speaker's linguistic competence, is supplemented, or rather superseded by a schematic mythological convention internalized as a specific sexual script:
>
> | | |
> |---|---|
> | | (Normal = Neutral) |
> | GENITAL SIZE (MALE): | Gigantic = Good |
> | | Small = Bad |

GENITAL SIZE (MALE): Gigantic = Good

GENITAL SIZE (FEMALE): Gigantic = Bad
Normal = Neutral
(Small = Good?)

(The lines in parentheses do not seem to be of any use in sexual humour.)

References and further reading

Anonymous (1970): 'Effects of sexual activity on beard growth in man'. *Nature* (226) 869–70.

Armstrong, E.G. (1986): 'Country music sex songs: An ethnomusicological account'. *J. Sex Research* (22) 370–98.

Doering, C.H., Brodie, H.K.H., Kraemer, H.C., Becker, H. and Hamburg, D.A. (1974): 'Plasma testosterone levels and psychologic measures in men over a 2-month period'. *Sex Differences in Behavior*, 413–31, Wiley, NY.

Fox, C.A., Ismail, A.A.A., Love, D.N., Kirkham, D.E. and Loraine, J.A. (1972): 'Studies on the relationship between plasma testosterone levels and human sexual activity'. *J. Endocrinology* (52) 51–8.

Lee, P.A., Jaffe, R.B. and Midgley, A.R. Jr (1974): 'Lack of alteration of serum gonadatropins in men and women following sexual intercourse'. *American J. Obstet. Gynecol.* (120) 985–7.

Moyle, R.M. (1975): 'Sexuality in Samoan art forms'. *Archives of Sexual Behav.* (4) 227–47.

Pirke, K.M., Kockott, G. and Dittmar, F. (1974): 'Psychosexual stimulation and plasma testosterone in man'. *Archives of Sexual Behav.* (3) 577–84.

Raskin, V. (1984): *Semantic Mechanisms of Humour*. D. Reidel Publ. Co., Netherlands.

St Lawrence, J.S. and Joyner, D.J. (1991): 'The effects of sexually violent rock music on males' acceptance of violence against women'. *Psychology of Women Quarterly* (15) 49–63.

13

Deviations Various

Even before Gosselin (1979) took an interest in the personality characteristics of the average rubber fetishist, sexual deviation has been a source of constant inspiration to the scientist. We shall follow the accepted pattern of specializing in individual deviations and leave the reader to draw his or her own general conclusions.

Before proceeding, however, we must stress that no moral censure is necessarily implied by including any group under the heading 'Deviations'. A deviation is no more than a digression from the mode of behaviour adopted by the majority with or without the use of rubber goods, equipment or specialist clothing. Perversion (see chapter 14) is, of course, a more serious matter.

For any reader having difficulties separating the two categories, we may offer the following useful rule of thumb: Deviation is when you use a feather; perversion is when you use the whole chicken.

We hope this clarifies the matter.

Adultery and Incest

An Act of 1650 was passed in England 'for the suppressing of the abominable and crying sins of Incest, Adultery and Fornication, wherewith this land is much defiled and Almighty God highly displeased'. It specified the death penalty for incest and adultery, though a man could escape death for adultery if he did not know the woman was married; and a woman could escape if her husband had been absent for three years.

Fornication was punishable by three months in prison and a good behaviour bond for one year. Brothel-keepers, however, would be whipped, set in a pillory 'and there marked with a hot iron in the forehead with the letter "B" and then jailed for three years. Death for a second conviction.'

Three hundred and forty years later, Bellis and Baker (1990) examined the frequency of 'extra-pair copulations' (also known technically as a 'bit on the side') in human females on days 6–20 of the 28-day menstrual cycle to see whether, like many animals, the likelihood of conception influences choice of days for mating. 'The data support the sperm-competition theory of double-mating behaviour.'

Hansen (1987) looked at 'extradyadic relations' (EDR) during courtship and discovered that 70.9 per cent of males and 57.4 per cent of females either participate in EDR or know that their partner has been doing so. For males, it was the ones who had been dating for the longest time who were most likely to have an EDR, while for females EDR activity correlated with liberal sex attitudes, and 'non-traditional gender-role orientation'. They also did not go to church as much as girls who didn't screw around.

Bestiality

Pichel and Hart (1988) described a case-study in which a kitten was able to contribute significantly to sexual happiness. A couple (human male and human female) had been married for three years but had not developed any sexual intimacy. Since the couple seemed affectively allergic to physical contact, a systematic desensitization programme was designed for them, consisting of stroking and playing with their pet kitten. This had the effect of relaxing them,

Bestiality

curing their anxieties about physical contact and preparing them for more intimate contact with each other.

Exhibitionism

Kolarsky and Madlafousek (1983) had a bright idea about why flashers flash. Since such exhibitionists are known to be generally sexually arousable by normal female erotic behaviour, their problem seemed to be one of progressing normally from introductory sexual advances (pre-exposure) to the advanced sexual state of exposure.

To test the theory that exhibitionists have a problem of transition between such sexual motivational states, the experimenters persuaded groups of exhibitionists and non-exhibitionists to put on their penile tumescence gauges and watch some specially prepared dirty videos.

In the first phase of the experiment, they found that

exhibitionists are not aroused by female fear or anger, but are aroused by a female exposing her genitals, especially if she points at them too.

In the second phase, they discovered that a control group of non-exhibitionists were only aroused by the same genital-pointing females if they had been at least mildly erotically aroused immediately before. ('With no prestimulation, this behavior [females pointing at their exposed genitals] only weakened the effect.'

Exhibitionists, however, were less aroused by the female flashers if they had previously been stimulated by something milder.

Translating these results to the sexual behaviour of the exhibitionist, it seems that he has a problem in transition between the usual early (unexposed) stages of stimulation and the moment when the partners look at each other's genitals. The researchers therefore end with the following piece of advice: *'It may be useful to shape erotic partnership of exhibitionists along lines different from those traditionally prevalent in our cultures.'*

First look at each other's genitals, perhaps, then shake hands.

Fetishism: Rubber

Gosselin (1979) drew his experimental subjects from visitors to sex shops and members of rubber-fetishistic societies in the UK and US and gave them personality tests in order to establish what differentiated rubber fetishists from the general population. His conclusions were that:

> Rubberites are more impersonal and prudish, have higher frequency of sexual thoughts and more physical excitement attached to those thoughts, but are not significantly more introverted, neurotic (either generally or sexually), do not believe themselves to be more sexually excitable and are no less masculine than the control group.

On examining their biographical data, still more negative findings emerged, including the discoveries that the rubberite is not predominantly from small families, is not an only child, does not have a plethora of older sisters and has not been brought up by only one parent. He does not produce fewer children than average, nor is he more likely to divorce or separate.

He does, however, score higher than average on the 'lie-scale' of the Eysenck Personality Inventory, which is interpreted as signifying a high need for social acceptance.

One should, perhaps, be wary of reading too much into these results. Firstly, they depended on a volunteer sample of rubber fetishists and could therefore be typical not of the average rubber fetishist but of the average rubber fetishist who also likes filling out personality tests. Secondly, the high score on Eysenck's lie-scale could also indicate a high probability of motivational distortion in the other test results. In other words, they might all have been a pack of fibs.

Fetishism: Shoes

Epstein (1975) discusses the case of a fifteen-year-old boy who liked to play with wet canvas shoes. The boy's own description was: 'I like to take shoes and get them wet; I go around and ask all the ladies in the neighborhood to let me get their shoes and wet them.' Ideally he would also like the woman finally to put on high-heeled shoes.

His mother 'became concerned about his frequent wetting of shoes under faucet water and his importuning neighborhood ladies for their shoes' so took him to the doctor. After asking whether the psychiatrist's wife wore canvas shoes, and whether one of his secretaries would not mind, next time she came in, wearing wet canvas shoes, the patient asked to be furnished with a pair of black or red canvas shoes and a bucket for his next visit.

Despite providing the shoes and the bucket, and watching the patient's flushed reaction to the wettened shoes on the next visit, the psychiatrist could not provide a complete explanation of the wet-shoe fetish. 'The shoe captures his attention probably because of its linkage to a woman who had such a shoe and whose shoe became wet. The position in time of such an affectively laden memory could not be definitely established.'

Whatever the history behind it, the shoe had become a symbol of femininity:

> When the patient wets the shoe, he is effecting some type of union with a woman. The union may be coital in import, but other types of union may be symbolized. The patient's own foot is put into the shoe and by this act of union or incorporation, a basic human maneuver toward any object symbolically endowed with qualities of desirability, he becomes, or more properly, possesses, a woman.

Fetishism: Shoes

Curiously, Epstein (1969) goes for a much simpler explanation of a rubber boot being observed to evoke penile erection and ejaculation in a chimpanzee and erection in a baboon. In this case, the explanation is that the glistening rubber surface may bear a resemblance to the swollen skin around the genitals of an excited female of the species.

There is no suggestion that the chimpanzee might, at some time in his past, have known a female chimpanzee who wore rubber boots.

McCully (1976), discussing the same case of the boy canvas-shoe wetter, emphasizes the archetypal nature of the shoe as fetish object as exemplified in *Cinderella*.

> The glass slipper became numinous for the prince, both as a practical means of searching for the owner and because it contained his projections in lieu of the owner . . . The glass slipper symbolizes the woman-as-container, something magic that constellated the young prince's whole being, including phallic aspirations.

With Cinderella's step-sisters symbolic of natural unrelatedness, she found herself unrelated to negative matriarchal power (the step-mother), but had the compensating advantage of being in a good relationship with nurturant matriarchal power (fairy godmother). 'Because of this, she possessed all that was necessary to constellate the young prince's anima, or relatedness.'

What McCully does not say, however, is that after marrying the foot-fetishistic prince, Cinderella, far from living happily ever after, may well find that his coach (an obvious symbol of sexuality) turns into a pumpkin at midnight.

Lesbianism

Lieh-Mak, O'Hoy and Luk (1983) make some interesting observations about the history and present nature of lesbianism in China and Hong Kong. 'Although lesbianism is known in China, the literature is scanty. On the other hand, the literature of male homosexuality is considerable.'

In this connection, they mention the term *Tuan-hsiu* (the cut sleeve) used to denote homosexuality. The term originated from a tale of the Emperor Ai-ti (reigned 6–1 B.C.) who cut off a sleeve from a favourite garment rather than disturb the sleep of a favourite lover who was lying on it.*

Anyway, in ancient China concubines were an important symbol of wealth and power. 'A duke can take nine concubines at one time, an emperor can take twelve concubines at one time', said the *Kung-yang Tsuen*. But the *Li-Chi* (Book of Rites) states that 'until the age of fifty, a husband should enter the pleasure pavilion of his wife once every third day, and of his concubines once every fifth day'.

As Lieh-Mak, O'Hoy and Luk point out:

> The number of concubines made this prescription a physical impossibility. The lack of sexual outlet, the social isolation and the close proximity of women made the harem a fertile ground for the development of lesbian relationships . . . In addition to pudendal contact, clitoral stimulation and cunnilingus, the use of artificial penises was also favoured . . . A double-ended dildo with two loops of silk cord in the middle was also used to enable both partners to obtain simultaneous pleasure.

They also quote a passage from a chapter by the legendary Yellow Emperor:

> Lady Precious Yin and Mistress White Jade lay on top of each other, their legs entwined so that their jade gates pressed together. They then moved in a rubbing and twisting fashion against each other like fishes gobbling flies or water plants from the surface. As they become more excited, the 'mouths' widen . . .

*It might be conjectured that the English term 'shirt-lifter' has a similarly romantic derivation.

And the next thing that happens in the story makes it clear that all that particular bit of lesbianism was for was to prepare the young ladies for the entrance of the Great Lord Yang who now thrusts between them. The preliminary rubbing and grinding helped preserve him from the 'Five Overstrainings'.

But that is all in the past. In two years of hunting in Hong Kong, the current researchers could find only fifteen women who would admit to being lesbians. They comprised four skilled factory workers, two nurses, two prison officers, one lawyer, one university teacher, one high school teacher, one advertising executive, one midwife, one fashion designer and one Buddhist nun. Several of these were adopted, or had parents who would have preferred them to be boys.

Their average age of first homosexual experience was 20.8 and none of them ever practised cunnilingus.

Rapists*

Marshall (1988) gathered information on 106 psychiatric patients who had been guilty of sexual crimes. The results were analysed according to type of crime, but sadly there were too few homosexual incest offenders, exhibitionists, voyeurs, mixed voyeur-exhibitionists or assaultive fetishists for any meaningful results to be obtained for those categories.

It was found, however, that rapists are generally brighter than child molesters.

This is particularly interesting when taken in conjunction with the findings of Ruff, Templer and Ayers (1976) who gave IQ tests to 136 convicted male felons at the Kentucky State Penitentiary. For the purposes of the analysis, they divided the subjects into three groups, according to whether

*We must stress that the disclaimer at the beginning of the chapter stressing that no moral censure is necessarily implied does not necessarily apply to this section.

they had been convicted of rape, other violent crime, or non-violent crime.

The rapists scored significantly lower on intelligence tests than either of the other two groups.

It could, of course, be that rapists who end up in jail are less intelligent than rapists who end up in psychiatric care, but further research is clearly needed on this interesting topic.

Sado-Masochism

Gosselin, Wilson and Barrett (1991) gave personality questionnaires to a sample of sado-masochistic women. They discovered that sado-masochists are more extroverted, more stable, lower in neuroticism and higher in psychoticism than the average woman. Both in sexual fantasies and behaviour, they were more active than average, but there were no signs of general lesbian tendencies or that they despised men.

The conclusion was that such women indulge in sado-masochistic practices because they and their partners like it.

On the question of sado-masochism in males, several studies and anecdotal evidence suggest that the submissive role is far more prevalent than a need to dominate. Xaviera Hollander ('The Happy Hooker') claimed that 90 per cent of her clients who purchased sado-masochistic equipment preferred to be on the

Ninety per cent of her clients preferred to be on the receiving end

receiving end, a figure that was very much in line with the research of Janus, Bess and Saltus (1977).

Their survey of prostitutes catering to the rich and powerful in Washington revealed that requests to be beaten outnumbered requests to inflict beating by a factor of eight to one.

The only recent study which has failed to produce a majority for submissives over dominators was that of Spengler (1977) whose survey indicated about equal numbers. But that study was restricted to Germans.

Revealing insights into the true nature of the relationship between masochists and pain were obtained by Scott (1983) and Weinberg, Williams and Moser (1984) who showed that masochists dislike going to the dentist and suffering headaches just as much as anyone else.

Sodomy

We can do no better here than to refer the reader to the excellent special double issue of the *Journal of Homosexuality* (16) 1988 nos 1 and 2, entitled: *The pursuit of sodomy: Male homosexuality in Renaissance and Enlightenment Europe.*

Papers for this special issue included the following:

Boon, L.J.: 'Those damned sodomites: Public images of sodomy in the eighteenth-century Netherlands.'

Dall'Orto, G.: ' "Socratic Love" as a disguise for same-sex love in the Italian Renaissance.'

Huussen, A.H.: 'Persecution of sodomy in eighteenth-century Frisia, Netherlands.'

Morris, P.: 'Sodomy and male honor: The case of Somerset 1740–50.'

Noordam, D.J.: 'Sodomy in the Dutch Republic 1600–1725.'

Oosterhoff, J.: 'Sodomy at sea and at the Cape of Good Hope during the eighteenth century.'

Perry, M.E.: 'The "nefarious sin" in early modern Seville.'

Rey, M.: 'Police and sodomy in eighteenth-century Paris: from sin to disorder.'

Streakley, J.D.: 'Sodomy in enlightenment Prussia: From execution to suicide.'
Trumbach, R.: 'Sodomitical assaults, gender role and sexual development in eighteenth-century London.'
Van Rosen, W.: 'Sodomy in early modern Denmark: A crime without victims.'

Transsexualism

According to Lindgren and Pauly (1975): 'The transsexual is unable to form a satisfactory body image because of the dissonance between his or her anatomical sex and gender identity (psychological sex). The reality of the transsexual's body does not conform to the preferred and desired body image.' Which is why they then present themselves for sex-change surgery, thereby presenting a problem to the medical profession.

Lindgren and Pauly's research identified the Body Image Scale as a potentially useful tool in evaluating such requests. The basis of the form is a list of thirty body parts, for each of which the respondent is asked to rate his or her satisfaction on a 5-point scale: Very satisfied, Satisfied, Neutral, Dissatisfied, Very dissatisfied.

The body parts are nose, shoulders, hips, chin, calves, breasts, hands, adam's apple, scrotum (or vagina), height, thighs, arms, eyebrows, penis (or clitoris), waist, muscles, buttocks, facial hair, face, weight, biceps, testicles (or ovaries-uterus), hair, voice, figure, body hair, chest, appearance, stature.

They found that male transsexuals, before treatment, were most dissatisfied with their body hair, facial hair, testicles, scrotum and penis, with hips, voice and figure not far behind. Female transsexuals, however, were most dissatisfied with their chest, facial hair, ovaries-uterus, clitoris, vagina and breasts, all just ahead of voice.

Another important finding about transsexuals was that of Barr and Blaszczynski (1976) who measured the penile volume changes and galvanic skin responses of groups of transsexuals, homosexuals and heterosexuals as they watched film sequences depicting naked men and women.

> Student controls [heterosexuals] and homosexuals showed significantly greater galvanic skin responses to the preferred than to the nonpreferred sex. Transsexuals tended to show larger galvanic skin responses to females than did male homosexuals. No strong relationships were found between penile volume and galvanic skin responses to the preferred sex. It is concluded that transsexual patients differ significantly from homosexual patients in autonomic responsivity, which may have diagnostic usefulness.

Voyeurism

Gebhard, Gagnon, Pomeroy and Christenson analysed various groups of sex offenders, including a group of voyeurs whom they characterized as 'persevering optimists', rather like

> ardent fishermen, undaunted by failure and always hoping that the next time their luck will be better. Just as the fisherman will wait patiently for hours, so will the peeper wait for a female to finish some interminable minor chores before going to bed – and then, like as not, she may turn off the light before undressing.

Voyeurs were found to have more sado-masochistic, bestial and otherwise bizarre (undefined) masturbatory fantasies, and married voyeurs engaged more in both fellatio and cunnilingus with extramarital partners, but no more than average with their wives. Their fear of venereal disease was higher than normal. They did not gamble, drink or use drugs to excess and were generally considered the most mentally healthy of sex offenders.

Wife-Swapping

According to Spanier and Cole (1975): 'A theoretical formulation argues that swinging [mate-swapping] is a form of extra-marital sexual activity which serves to define as good and acceptable a behavior that in other forms and in the past has been considered deviant or immoral.'

So, bearing in mind the fact that Smith and Smith (1970) had demonstrated that swingers were not especially neurotic or deviant in other aspects of their married or family life, they interviewed 579 married adults in the Midwest of the United States.

When asked whether they agreed or disagreed with the statement, 'Wife swapping is wrong', those who agreed were generally better off, older, longer married, better maritally adjusted and went to church more often than those who disagreed.

When asked whether they agreed or disagreed with the statement, 'Wife swapping can have positive effects on husband–wife relationships', those who agreed were generally less well educated, maritally less well-adjusted and went to church less frequently than those who disagreed.

Most respondents disapproved of mate-swapping, and only 6.7 per cent said they would consider doing it if they had the chance. The actual figure for those who had done so was 2 per cent of the total sample.

References and further reading

Barr, R. and Blaszczynski, A. (1976): 'Autonomic respones of transsexual and homosexual males to erotic film sequences'. *Archives of Sexual Behav.* (5) 211–22.

Bellis, M.A. and Baker, R.R. (1990): 'Do females promote sperm competition? Data for humans'. *Animal Behavior* (4) 997–9.

Bellwether, J. (1982): 'Love means never having to say oops: a Lesbian's guide to s/m safety'. In *Samois: Coming to Power* (69–79), Alyson, Boston.
Epstein, A.W. (1969): Fetishism: A comprehensive view. In Masserman, J.H. (Ed), *Science and Psychoanalysis*, vol. 15. Grune and Stratton, NY.
Epstein, A.W. (1975): 'The fetish object: Phylogenetic considerations'. *Archives of Sexual Behav.* (4) 303–8.
Gebhard, P., Gagnon, J., Pomeroy, W. and Christenson, C. (1965): *Sex Offenders (An Analysis of Types)*. Harper and Row, NY.
Gosselin, C.C. (1979): 'Personality attributes of the average rubber fetishist'. In Cook, M. and Wilson, G. (Eds), *Love and Attraction – An International Conference (Swansea 1977)*. Pergamon Press.
Gosselin, C.C., Wilson, G.D. and Barrett, P.T. (1991): 'The personality and sexual preferences of sado-masochistic women'. *Personality and Individual Differences* (912) 11–15.
Hansen, G.L. (1987): 'Extradyadic relations during courtship'. *J. Sex Research* (23) 382–90.
Janus, S., Bess, B. and Saltus, C. (1977): *A Sexual Profile of Men in Power*. Prentice Hall, Englewood Cliffs, NJ.
Kamel, G.W.L. (1980): 'Leathersex: Meaningful aspects of gay sado-masochism'. *Deviant Behavior* (1) 171–91.
Kolarsky, A. and Madlafősek, J. (1983): 'The inverse role of preparatory erotic stimulation in exhibitionists: Phallometric studies. *Archives of Sexual Behav.* (12) 123–33.
Lieh-Mak, S., O'Hoy, K.M. and Luk, S.L. (1983): 'Lesbianism in the Chinese of Hong Kong'. *Archives of Sexual Behav.* (12) 21–30.
Lindgren, T.W. and Pauly, Ira (1975): 'A body-image scale for evaluating transsexuals'. *Archives of Sexual Behav.* (4) 639–56.
Lucy, J. (1982): 'If I ask you to tie me up will you still want to love me?' In *Samois: Coming to Power*, Alyson, Boston.
McCully, R.S. (1976): 'A Jungian commentary on Epstein's case (wet-shoe fetish)'. *Archives of Sexual Behav.* (5) 185–8.
Marshall, W.L. (1988): 'The use of sexually explicit stimuli by rapists, child molesters and non-offenders'. *J. Sex Research* (25).
Pichel, C.H. and Hart, L.A. (1988): 'Desensitization of sexual anxiety: Relaxation, play and touch experience with a pet'. *Anthrozoos* (2) 58–61.
Ruff, C.F., Templer, D.I. and Ayers, J.L. (1976): 'The

intelligence of rapists'. *Archives of Sexual Behav.* (5) 327–9.
Scott, G.G. (1983): *Erotic Power: An Exploration of Dominance and Submission*. Citadel Press, Secaucus, NJ.
Smith, J.R. and Smith, L.G. (1970): 'Co-marital sex and the sexual freedom movement'. *J. Sex Research* (6) 131–42.
Spanier, G.B. and Cole, C.L. (1975): 'Mate swapping: Perceptions, value orientations and participation in a Midwestern community'. *Archives of Sexual Behav.* (4) 143–59.
Spengler, A. (1977): 'Manifest sado-masochism of males: Results of an empirical study'. *Archives of Sexual Behav.* (6) 441–56.
Weinberg, M.S., Williams, C.J. and Moser, C. (1984): 'The social constituents of sado-masochism'. *Social Problems* (31) 379–89.

14

Perversions

Glass or ceramic

bottles and jars	31
bottle with rope attached	1
glass or cup	12
light bulb	7
tube	6

Food

apple	1
banana	2
carrot	4
cucumber	3
onion	2
parsnip	1
plantain with condom	1
potato	1
salami	1
turnip	1
zucchini	2

Wooden

ax handle	1
stick or broom handle	10
miscellaneous/unspecified	3

Sexual device

vibrator	23
dildo	15

Kitchen equipment

blunt knife	1
ice pick	1
knife sharpener	1
mortar pestle	2
plastic spatula	1
spoon	1
tin cup	1

Miscellaneous

bottle cap	1
cattle horn	3
frozen pig's tail	1
kangaroo tumour	1
plastic rod	1
stone	2
toothbrush holder	1
toothbrush package	1
whip handle	2

Tools

candle	1
flashlight	2
iron rod	1
pen	2
rubber tube	1
screwdriver	1
toothbrush	1
wire spring	1

Inflated object

balloon	1
balloon attached to cylinder	1
condom	1

Balls

baseball	2
tennis ball	1

Containers

baby powder can	1
candle box	1
snuff box	1

Collections

2 glass tubes
72.5 jewellers saws
oil can with peanut stopper
piece of wood and peanut
umbrella handle and enema tubing
2 glasses
phosphorous match ends
402 stones
toolbox
2 bars of soap
beer glass and preserving pot
lemon and cold cream jar
2 apples
spectacles, suitcase key, tobacco pouch and magazine

That was not, as you might perhaps surmise, a rather eccentric wedding list, but the complete collection, according to Busch and Starling (1986) of references in medical literature to the surgical removal of foreign bodies inserted into the rectum.

> Voluntary self-insertions occurred in 195 incidents involving men and 7 involving women (28:1 male to female ratio). Foreign body insertion into women is often by the vaginal route, which would appear to offer advantages over the rectal route in control, comfort, distensibility, sensation, strength and lubricity.

Some of the objects listed above were the result of assault

(including the phosphorus match heads and the collection of spectacles, suitcase key, tobacco pouch and magazine), others were probably inserted by a consenting partner, but the majority appear to be the results of self-insertion.

When encountering patients with objects stuck up their rectums, according to Busch and Starling, 'No purpose is served by humiliating the distressed patient. Embarrassment and fear of humiliation may explain frequent reports of patients admitted with rectal foreign bodies who give vague and non-specific histories.'

Reported explanations include inserting the object for relief of haemorrhoids, relief of constipation and relief of itching. In all cases, the doctor should adopt the manner advised by Haft, Benjamin and Zeit (1974) in their paper on foreign bodies in the vagina: '*Such patients should be treated with the utmost concern and tact, keeping in mind the great embarrassment they feel*'.

And in case you are wondering, the toolbox was found inside a convict and contained saws and other items for a planned escape attempt, and the kangaroo tumour was a pedunculated perianal skin tumour.

References and further reading

Busch, D.B. and Starling, J.R. (1986): 'Rectal foreign bodies: Case reports and a comprehensive review of the world's literature'. *Surgery* (100) 512–18.

Haft, J.S. and Benjamin, H.B. (1973): 'Foreign bodies in the rectum: Some psychosexual aspects'. *Medical Aspects of Human Sexuality* (7) 74–95.

Haft, J.S., Benjamin, H.B. and Zeit, W. (1974): 'Foreign bodies in the female genitourinary tract: Some psychosexual aspects'. *Medical Aspects of Human Sexuality* (8) 54–78.

Panasci, E.H. and Zutrauen, H.A. (1956): 'A cucumber perforating rectosigmoid junction'. *American J. Proctology* (7) 230–2.

Smiley, O. (1919): 'A glass tumbler in the rectum'. *J. American Med. Ass.* (72) 1285.

15

Athletes and Bearded Women

We begin this final chapter with perhaps the most important underlying question of all, yet one which is notoriously difficult to answer: Is sex good for you? The very phrasing of the question, of course, depends on such metaphysical and moralistic concerns such as What is Good? And, is Evil so bad after all? Yet that is not to say that we cannot tackle some aspects of it.

In Gordon (1988) the question was approached peripherally in a study that set out to determine not whether sex was good for sportsmen, but to what extent sports coaches believed it was harmful.

Once again (see chapter 8), Onan is held to account unjustly. In his book *Onanisme*, first published in 1758, the Swiss physician Tissot claimed that 'the loss of an ounce of semen would weaken more than that of 40 ounces of blood'. For semen was the stuff of divine energy.

That view was generally maintained until the present century, and there are still widespread beliefs that sex can affect athletic prowess. Gordon quotes the commonly uttered coaches' maxim 'Girls give you weak legs', to support his contention that 'Athletics . . . may be the last bastion of ancient views of spermatic conservation.'

Johnson (1968) did what was apparently the first serious study on the subject, giving fourteen married ex-athletes a 'maximum effort grip strength endurance test' both on a morning after they had had sex and on a morning after they had abstained for six days. No differences were found in their performance levels.

Twenty years after that study, Gordon wanted to see to what extent baseball and basketball coaches still believed that sex was not advisable before a game. Accordingly, he sent questionnaires to the head coaches of one hundred clubs in each sport of whom 65 per cent responded by filling in their answers.

The questions began with some items on general coaching philosophy before getting down to the important matter: 'Do you feel that having sexual relations the night or morning before a game negatively affects athletic performance?'

Only 8.6 per cent of the respondents said yes, 50 per cent said no, and 41.4 per cent were don't knows. The experimenter had hypothesized that older coaches would be more likely to believe sex to be harmful, but that hypothesis was not supported by the results. There was, however, a significant tendency for religious coaches, particularly if they were Catholic, to believe that sex was bad for you.

The coaches were also asked: 'Do you believe that there are any positive consequences associated with having sex the night or morning before the game?'

13 per cent said yes, 76 per cent said no, and 10 per cent didn't know.

Most revealing of all, however, were the answers given when the coaches who viewed sex as harmful were asked to explain in what way it could negatively affect performance.

Seven coaches felt that it reduced concentration; seven felt that it reduced muscle strength; six thought that it reduced aggressiveness; four believed that it reduced the will to win; and one said: *'It is not the sex that is harmful, it is the finding it that wears them down'*.

We move from athletes to the question of women's body hair.

Basow (1991) sent a questionnaire to over 200 American

women members of the National Women's Studies Association and the American Psychological Association to ask them if they regularly shaved their legs and/or armpits, whether they had ever done so, how long they had been doing so, and why they did, or did not, do so. The response rate was 56 per cent.

Eighty per cent of the sample did remove their leg and/or underarm hair at least occasionally.

Eighty-five per cent had begun removing their hair by the age of fourteen.

There were two main categories of reasons for doing it: femininity/attractiveness or social/normative (i.e. to look pretty or because it is the expected behaviour).

Most begin shaving for social/normative reasons, but continue doing it for reasons of femininity/attractiveness. The most common reasons for starting were:

1 It was the thing to do
2 Women are supposed to shave
3 It made me feel grown up
4 People would look at me funny if I didn't

The most common reasons for continuing to shave were:

1 I like the soft, silky feeling
2 It makes me feel attractive
3 It is the thing to do
4 People would look at me funny if I didn't

One of the points of the research, however, was to discover whether there was a difference between heterosexual and lesbian women in shaving behaviour.

'Norms for female attractiveness implicitly or explicitly revolve around attracting men. Therefore it is predicted that women who are not trying to attract men (i.e. lesbians) will be less likely to conform to the norm than other women.'

Accordingly, they were also asked questions about their feminist beliefs and sexual tendencies.

Women who do not shave are likely to be feminists

'The large majority of women who did not shave their legs identified as strong feminists (75.5 per cent of non-shavers) and/or not exclusively heterosexual (64.2 per cent of non-shavers).'

The main reasons given by the feminist and/or lesbian non-shavers were described as political, such as 'women's bodies are fine as they are' or 'shaving is stupid'.

Despite this, however, non-shavers are still in a minority (28 per cent) even among very strong feminists.

One conclusion to be plucked from this research is therefore that women who do not shave legs and/or armpits are likely to be feminists and/or lesbians, but the average feminist/lesbian is still more likely to shave than not.

But if you asked a lesbian to draw a picture of a woman, would she draw one with hairy legs? That was one question not answered in Przybyla, Byrne and Allgeier (1988) in their remarkable study of the effects of sexual attitude on human figure drawing.

For the purposes of their experiment, they had 17 male and 23 female undergraduates fill in a Sexual Opinion Survey and draw pictures of naked men and women. Their hypothesis was that those with positive sexual attitudes (erotophiles) would be more likely to include explicit genitals on their pictures than subjects with negative sexual attitudes (erotophobes). 'In addition, it was hypothesized that erotophilia, in contrast with erotophobia, is associated with the drawing of proportionately larger sexual anatomy.'

So after everyone had drawn their pictures, two independent raters set about measuring the body parts of the sketches in millimetres. 'All physical characteristics were measured at their longest and widest points.'

The findings were generally, but not always, on the lines predicted: '*In drawing a male figure, male and female erotophiles were more likely than erotophobes to include a urethral opening, a glans and chest hair. In drawing a female figure, female erotophiles were more likely than female erotophobes to include pubic hair and nipples.*'

In drawing male figures, however, erotophilia–erotophobia seemed to have no influence on whether pubic hair, nipples, facial hair, ears or navel appeared in the drawing. And in drawing female figures, sexual attitudes did not correlate with the drawing of genital details, hair, ears or navel.

However, when it came down to precise measurements, some strong correlations were observed between erotophilia–erotophobia scores and details of the drawing. In the drawings by males, penis–body ratio, penis length, penis width, scrotum length and scrotum width in the pictures all correlated highly with erotophilia. Breast length and breast width were close behind.

In females' drawings, the strongest indicator of erotophilia was again penis–body ratio, with penis length, and penis width also highly correlated, but mons length and mons width coming in ahead of scrotum length as signs of erotophilic tendencies. Whereas breast length in females' pictures also correlated well with the erotophilia of the artist, breast width did less well.

One further interesting aspect mentioned by the researchers is the apparent anomaly when compared with a 1987 result of Kelley and Musialowski, who found that erotophobic males 'report that they possess longer penises than do erotophiles in reporting about themselves'.

If erotophobes pretend they have large penises, why then do they draw men with small ones? '*Possibly, the avoidance behavior that is suggested by the figure-drawing data is transformed into defensive over-compensation in describing one's own physical attributes.'*

In other words, they don't like thinking about penises, but if they have to talk about their own they're going to exaggerate to make them worth talking about.

Much of this book has carried the implicit message that sex would be far less hassle if one's sexual partners came with instruction manuals. Such an experiment has never been done, but Tanner and Pollack (1988) tried the same idea with condoms.

They divided 36 heterosexual couples into three groups:

Group 1 were given condoms with instructions on how they could be incorporated in various ways to enhance erotic foreplay; group 2 were given condoms without instructions; group 3 were not given any condoms.

They had all previously filled in a questionnaire in which their attitudes to condoms were assessed.

Two weeks later, they all came back and filled in the questionnaire again. Only the members of group 1 had a significantly enhanced attitude towards condoms.

And finally, two orgasmic research studies, one on technique, the other on male–female differences.

Eickel, de Simone and Kule (1988) investigated whether females' orgasmic responses could be enhanced by improving their partner's stimulation technique during intercourse. Their paper describes a coital alignment technique which combines the 'riding high' missionary procedure with 'genitally focussed pressure–counterpressure applied in the coordination of sexual movement'.

They taught the technique to 43 couples and compared their experiences, by means of a questionnaire, with those of 43 couples who had not been taught the technique.

The results showed significant differences between females in the two groups, with the experimental group (who had been taught the technique) higher on orgasmic attainment and simultaneous orgasm, as well as describing their orgasms as more 'complete' and 'satisfying'.

Which leaves us with the most important unanswered question: Can you tell the difference between male orgasms and female orgasms?

Vance and Wagner (1976) tackled this question in a delightfully rigorous way by asking around 300 student subjects to describe their orgasms in writing.

> Write a brief statement indicating what an orgasm feels like. If you have never had an orgasm, please describe how you think it would feel. Do not sign your name, but indicate your sex and whether your description of an orgasm is real or imagined by putting an R or an I on the paper. Limit your comments to at most one side of the paper.

They then incorporated a brilliant piece of experimental design by asking the subjects also to write, on the other side of the paper, what it feels like if you have eaten too much 'If you have never eaten too much, describe how you think it would feel . . .'

The reason for this was to eliminate people whose writing style was identifiably male or female. They gave the eating descriptions to another group of students

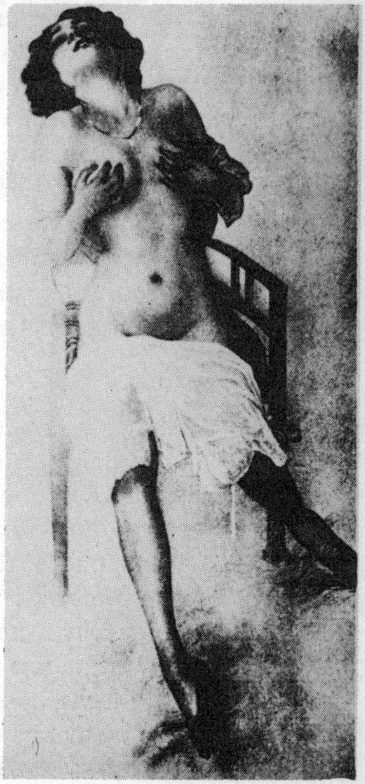

'If you have never had an orgasm, please describe how you think it would feel'

and asked them to judge whether each was written by a male or female. If too many judged the sex of the writer correctly, they excluded that writer from the orgasm survey.

They also eliminated the imagined orgasms and those whose descriptions were too short. From the remainder they picked 24 male and 24 female descriptions at random, modifying them where necessary to omit obvious clues to the gender of the writer. So the sexual giveaways of 'penis' and 'vagina' became 'genitals' and 'wife' or 'husband' or 'boyfriend' became 'my partner'.

The 48 resulting descriptions were then given to 70 judges, all of whom were obstetrician-gynaecologists, psychologists or medical students.

The judges were asked simply to say whether each of the 48 descriptions was written by a man or a woman. And the result was that they couldn't do it. Only one of the seventy judges performed significantly better than chance, and this despite the fact that orgasm number 8 in their list contained a female giveaway in the phrase 'and then if the lovemaking is continued it repeats again and again'.

Even with this free point for a multiple orgasm, the average of the 70 judges was only 25.36 correct, compared with a chance score of 24.

Of the three groups, gynaecologist-obstetricians, psychologists and medical students, the psychologists did worst of all.

References and further reading

Basow, S.A. (1991): 'The hairless ideal: Women and their body hair'. *Psychology of Women Quarterly* (15) 83–96.

Eickel, E.W., de Simone, J. and Kule, S. (1988): 'The technique of coital alignment and its relation to female orgasmic response and simultaneous orgasm'. *J. Sex and Marital Ther.* (3) 129–41.

Gordon, M. (1988): 'College coaches' attitudes toward pre-game sex'. *J. Sex Research* (24) 256–62.

Johnson, W.R. (1968): 'Muscular performance following coitus'. *J. Sex Research* (4) 247–8.

Przybyla, D.P.J., Byrne, D. and Allgeier, E. (1988): 'Sexual attitudes as correlates of sexual details in human figure drawing'. *Archives of Sexual Behav.* (17) 99–105.

Tanner, W.M. and Pollack, R.H. (1988): 'The effect of condom use and erotic instructions on attitudes towards condoms'. *J. Sex Research* (25) 537–41.

Vance, E.B. and Wagner, N.N. (1976): 'Written descriptions of orgasm: A study of sex differences'. *Archives of Sexual Behav.* (5) 87–98.

Index